Laboratory Design Guide

For clients, architects and their design team

The laboratory design process from start to finish

Brian Griffin
B Arch (Syd) FRAIA MDIA ARIBA

Architect and Laboratory Design Consultant

Architectural Press
OXFORD   BOSTON   JOHANNESBURG   MELBOURNE   NEW DELHI   SINGAPORE

Architectural Press
An imprint of Butterworth-Heinemann
Linacre House, Jordan Hill, Oxford OX2 8DP
A division of Reed Educational and Professional Publishing Ltd
225 Wildwood Avenue, Woburn, MA 01801-2041

A member of the Reed Elsevier plc group

First published 1998

© Reed Educational and Professional Publishing Ltd 1998

British Library Cataloguing in Publication Data
Griffin, Brian
  Laboratory design guide
  1 Laboratories – Design
  1 Title
  727.5

Library of Congress Cataloguing in Publication Data
Griffin, Brian, B Arch (Syd) FRAIA MDIA ARIBA
  Laboratory design guide: for clients, architects and their design team:
  the laboratory design process from start to finish/Brian Griffin.
  Includes bibliographical references and index.
  ISBN 0 7506 3858 3
  1. Laboratories – Design and construction.   1.   Title.
  TH4652.G75   97–43246
  726'.5–dc21   CIP

ISBN 0 7506 3858 3

Designed and Typeset by ☎ Tek-Art, Croydon, Surrey
Printed and bound in Great Britain by Biddles of Kings Lynn and Guildford

FOR EVERY TITLE THAT WE PUBLISH, BUTTERWORTH-HEINEMANN
WILL PAY FOR BTCV TO PLANT AND CARE FOR A TREE.

Cover: Design for an interstitial services space between external walls and sunshading screen. Lawrence Nield &
Partners Australia, in association with Grose Bradley Architects and Brian Griffin Laboratory design consultant.

I dedicate this book to the client who gave me the inspiration to develop designs for maximum flexibility in laboratories.

Professor Ian Thornton

Dr Allan Marshall

Dr Allan Wright

Peter Berry

Department of Zoology, La Trobe University, Australia

Contents

Chapter 8 – Maintenance 69

Case studies 73

This is a selection of laboratory buildings and projects including university teaching and research, product quality assurance, research and development, testing laboratories, pathology services and medical research.

Appendices

Acknowledgements

I would like to thank the following for their encouragement and professional advice.

Caroline Langley BSc M Safety Sc Grad Dipl Occup Hygiene MSIA, Health, Safety and Environment Adviser, Tasmania. Commonwealth Scientific Industrial and Research Organisation (CSIRO Australia)

Dr Trevor N. Lockyer MSc PhD (UNSW), Manager, Corporate Facilities Management, ACTEW Corporation Ltd. (Australian Capital Territory Electricity and Water)

Neil Hanson BSc(Arch) Syd B Arch(Hons) Syd, Lawrence Nield & Partners, Australia Pty Ltd, Architects

Greg James Assoc Dip Sc (Bldg), Construction Superintendent, Engineering, Australian Nuclear Science & Technology Organisation (ANSTO)

Heather Turner B Appl Sc Dip Ind Chem Dip App Biol Cert Lab Saf, Safety Co-ordinator, State Chemistry Laboratory Agriculture, Victoria

Jeffrie Crosbie BSc (Hons) Syd, Operations Manager, Centenary Institute of Cancer Medicine and Cell Biology

Introduction

As the title suggests this book will guide clients, laboratory staff, architects, engineering consultants and project construction managers through the design process for a laboratory project.

The following represents an approach to the design of laboratory buildings, particularly the interior layout and furniture, which I have developed as a specialist laboratory design consultant.

As I believe that safety in laboratories is one of the most important design criteria, I became involved in the Australian Standard AS 2982 'Laboratory Design and Construction' as a committee member representing the Australian Institute of Architects.

I also lecture on this subject and always stress the importance of the safety aspects in laboratory design.

Another important design criterion is the ergonomics of the workplace to provide the best possible working environment for the laboratory staff. In the past scientists have been frustrated by their old facilities. Their efficiency is impaired and their fixed benches are like a straitjacket! So laboratory facilities should be designed for maximum flexibility in arranging the equipment and movable workbenches. With the assistance of a specialist joinery company, KPD Pty Limited, I have designed a laboratory furniture product, Space Lab, now manufactured in Australia and Europe. Feedback from completed installations over the past ten years has provided invaluable user advice for improving the furniture product.

Equipment and instrumentation manufacturers try to keep up with changes in laboratory practice. As facility designers we also have to respond to the new requirements.

I have used some of my commissions to illustrate my design philosophy and methodology. The examples selected are designs which were not compromised by site, building or other constraints.

I have also included a number of case studies to illustrate the designs by other architects who have described their design solutions to a variety of briefs and contributed their drawings and photographs.

Regulations and standards are being revised continually so I have not referred to these documents as they could be misleading. You must obtain the current editions. Likewise laboratory equipment, water and gas fittings are continually being improved by their manufacturers, so I have not included any technical data. Manufacturers are very willing to supply their current trade literature.

While laboratory regulations/standards and laboratory products/equipment are changing and vary from country to country, good design principles are universal and are the subject of this book.

I have included a selection of laboratory bibliography which represents a progressive development in laboratory design since the research into laboratory facilities sponsored by the Nuffield Foundation. We have now progressed beyond the designs described and illustrated in those texts to keep up with the ever changing requirements of scientific work, facility planning, science equipment, standards and regulations for our laboratory clients today and their prophesies for the future.

I have not included special-purpose laboratories as the client will be a specialist, will be fully informed on the requirements, and the brief will be more prescriptive than for the general laboratories.

While Chapter 1 is principally directed to the Laboratory Client and Chapters 2–8 are directed to the Design and Construction Team, everybody should benefit by reading all the parts.

Chapter 1

Design brief

1.1 Initiating the brief

The brief for a new laboratory or laboratory alterations is the description of the owner/users' requirements. This brief, known as the program in the USA, should be as complete as possible or there will be serious consequences later, in terms of arguments, extra costs and redesign, even reconstruction.

As an architect and laboratory design consultant, I generally find my clients have been waiting a long time for their new laboratory and cannot believe that the project has really been funded. So they are not well motivated to find time in their busy work schedule to prepare a complete brief.

A good technique I use to extract the information is to show examples of laboratory briefs I have received from other clients and which have been successful. These examples jog their memory and prompt contradictions which lead them to formulate their own brief.

I cannot stress too much the need to impress on those responsible for the brief the importance of their task. It has been said so often, because it is so true, that the building design is only as good as the brief.

To avoid overwhelming your staff with a huge questionnaire, start the process by having them summarise staff lists, description of laboratory type and function. Meet to review that summary and then build on it with more and more detail until you have a complete document of all your requirements.

1.2 Rationalisation

The laboratory environment is one of those work places where rationalisation can create a reasonable, safe, orderly arrangement of furniture and spaces.

If the brief is prepared by asking each member of the laboratory to state their individual requirements and then passing all this information to the laboratory designer to incorporate into the building, you may satisfy the existing staff but are unlikely to satisfy any new staff. Alterations to the laboratory spaces and furniture to suit future staff will be costly. Extreme cases of individual choice can leave you with 'white elephants' that other staff cannot use.

By all means follow the first step above, but then somebody has to rationalise the various requirements. This operation needs diplomacy but a sense of resolve. A laboratory development committee can sometimes do this job with more authority and impartiality. Whoever undertakes this task may not realise all the options available in terms of new generation furniture and servicing systems. Better that the laboratory designer is introduced at this early stage, before the staff have their new dream laboratory space firmly entrenched in their mind.

So basically don't follow the individual with extraordinary requirements but seek a compromise which will satisfy most of the needs and will also suit the next staff to work in that facility.

Rationalisation does not have to take away the individual's right to choose for themselves. From my experience a successful technique was to show the laboratory staff a 'family' of compatible modular workstations and storage units from which they selected their individual needs. As this series of units had been designed to cater for a variety of laboratory functions the staff had no problem and there was no vexed process of rationalisation.

1.3 Type and function of the laboratory

The laboratory manager needs to describe the type and function of the laboratory in lay terms as the brief will be read by architects and engineering consultants who may not be familiar with all the scientific vocabulary. When writing the description, keep the reader in mind; you are not writing this for your colleagues.

Your description of the functions can take the form of a workflow – for example, in a pathology laboratory: receive specimens, record data and relabel specimen, load into trays, separate in centrifuge, reload in separate trays, distribute to laboratory departments, test specimens and report, return to data entry. Figure 1.1 shows a typical workflow diagram.

On the other hand, you may describe a procedure or practice which does not have a workflow but several associated functions. The description of the laboratory functions should be accompanied by a space relationship diagram, also known as a 'bubble diagram' (Figure 1.2). In your bubble diagram show a thick line between bubbles when functional spaces need to be directly adjacent, a medium line when spaces need to be close but not adjacent and a thin line when access by corridor is sufficient.

The design team will use the client's bubble diagram to arrange the various spaces in the most desirable relationship to one another.

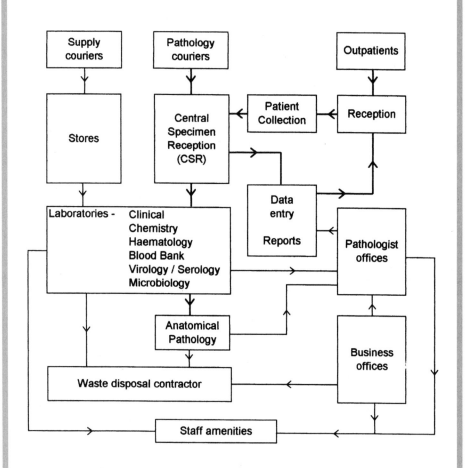

Figure 1.1 Workflow diagram showing the progress of specimens through a pathology laboratory

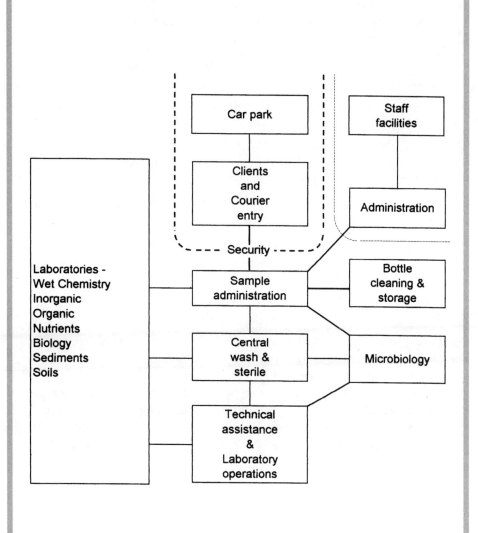

Figure 1.2 Space relationship diagram showing the various functional spaces and their desired relationships. The heavier line indicates the closer relationship

1.4 Staff

The list of the laboratory staff should include a brief job description of each member. Each staff member's responsibility will also be related to a functional space, so it will be necessary to decide if their write-up workstation is to be part of the functional laboratory space or separate, and how separate.

From my experience there seems to be three schools of thought when it comes to locating staff. The three locations are:

A. Adjacent to a dedicated laboratory workbench and generally at the window end of the bench (Figure 1.3), unless the workbench is a hazardous area.
B. Within the laboratory space but not immediately adjacent and partitioned, generally shared with other staff in the same laboratory (Figure 1.4).
C. Not within the laboratory group but separated by a dividing corridor (Figure 1.5).

Option A appears to be favoured by staff who are working on an individual project and who need to keep an eye on their work but which is not particularly hazardous.

Option B appears to be favoured by both staff and management. Staff feel they are close enough to their work and management feel that staff are safer if write-up time is not spent within the relatively hazardous laboratory environment. Management appear also to be wary of staff becoming too territorial, particularly if the function of the laboratory is quite dynamic and likely to change.

Option C appears to be favoured for the safest option and for energy conservation. The laboratory environmental requirements of controlled temperature, humidity and clean air cannot be achieved without high energy consumption. On the other hand, the office environmental requirements can be achieved with relatively low energy consumption, particularly if the architect designs the building envelope to the principles of passive energy, maximising solar energy and prevailing breezes (see 1.9 – Work environment).

From the point of view of occupational health and safety Option A is not recommended as it can never be guaranteed that the benchwork will not be hazardous.

1.5 Hazards

The hazards associated with the laboratory need to be clearly defined and should be listed with their location. Hazards in laboratories include the checklist under Appendix D and are generally the subject of standards and regulations which should be called up in the design brief, under each item.

Some hazardous laboratory operations will result in chemical waste, bio hazard waste, laboratory sharps, fumes and other by-products which need to be removed.

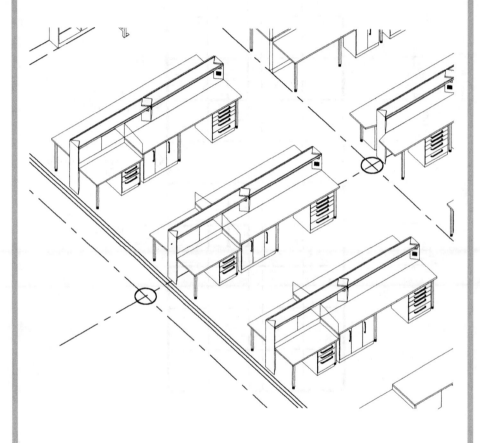

Figure 1.3 Individual write-up workstations at the window wall showing the desk level (750 mm) of the workstation and the protective screen to provide a measure of safety

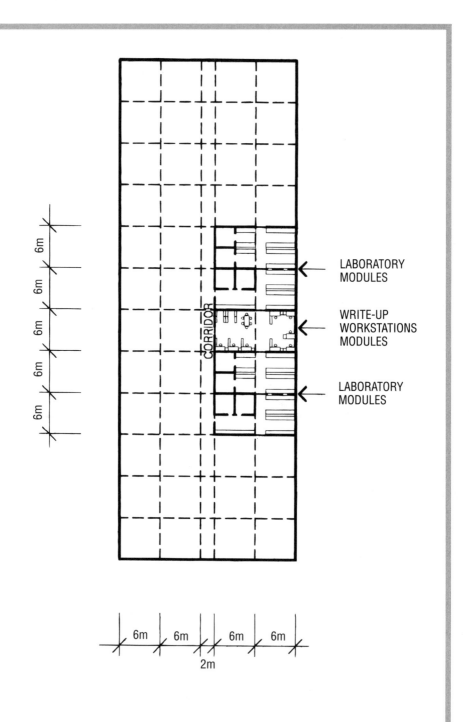

Figure 1.4 Grouped write-up workstations adjacent to the laboratories showing the close relationship but safe separation. The workstation module is the same size as the laboratory module so that they can be interchanged

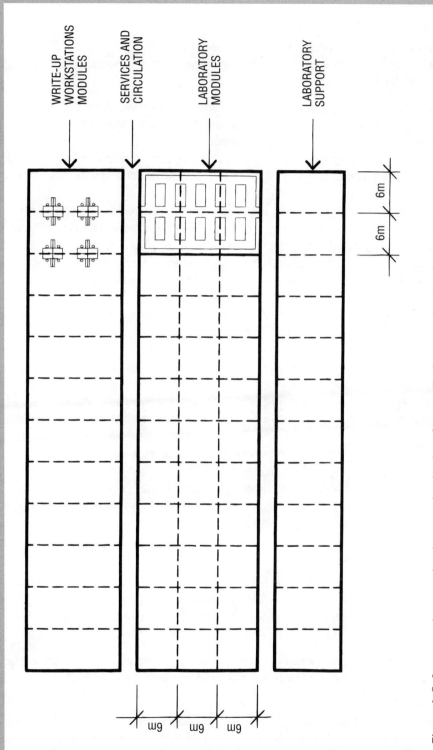

WRITE-UP
WORKSTATIONS
MODULES

SERVICES AND
CIRCULATION

LABORATORY
MODULES

LABORATORY
SUPPORT

6m 6m

6m 6m 6m

Figure I.5 Separate write-up workstations area showing the safest yet still adjacent relationship of workstations to laboratories

These wastes and their method of disposal need to be described in detail as provision will have to be made in the building design.

The following examples are by no means an exhaustive list of hazards but all laboratory users will know the particular hazards within their laboratory function and list them accordingly.

a. Procedures involving toxic, noxious, flammable and corrosive chemicals requiring the provision of a 'fume cupboard' to protect the operator from harmful airborne contaminants, splashing and minor explosions.
b. Procedures requiring a down-draught workbench, such as in anatomical dissection and decanting chemicals to exhaust the vapour downwards and away from the operator.
c. Laboratory procedures requiring protection of the operator from biological hazards such as bacteria, virus, pathogens, etc. and provision of a 'biological safety cabinet'.
d. Procedures, typically in pharmaceutical manufacturing laboratories, which require a supply of clean air where a product can be handled without fear of contamination. This is the function of a 'laminar flow cabinet'. These procedures can also be carried out in a 'clean room'.
e. Flammable liquids to be stored within the laboratory requiring the provision of a 'flammable liquids safety cabinet'. The estimated maximum volume of litres/m^2 needs to be given in the brief as it will have considerable effect on the 'hazard rating' of the laboratories and the maximum allowable floor area for each hazard rated laboratory.
f. Corrosive chemicals to be stored within the laboratory are a hazard to instruments and other equipment. The requirements should be for an externally ventilated cupboard.
g. Equipment which tests the compressive or tensile strength of materials and which could propel part or all of the equipment or materials being tested, requires special benches with screens to protect the operator.
h. High voltage equipment with its special operator protective requirements.
i. Procedures involving radioactive materials.
j. Radiation, ionising and non-ionising.
k. Visitors to the laboratory are a hazard to staff, equipment and themselves.

Remember that a hazard will be recognised as such by staff who are familiar with it, but may not be by visitors or new staff. The laboratory owner has a legal duty of care to staff and visitors. Visitors should always be accompanied by staff designated in the visitors' book at the security entry desk.

If visitors should not be exposed to particular unsafe procedures or hazards it will be necessary to contain these hazards within a 'restricted area', clearly signed 'No entry unless authorised'.

Another approach is to have a visitors' gallery overlooking the laboratories for public relations, particularly educational but also to provide a positive physical barrier to protect visitors.

The importance of considering the employer's duty of care to visitors cannot be overstressed and needs to be addressed in the brief.

1.6 Work space, benches and services

The design brief should list the various areas of accommodation. Some areas will be quite simply an office for an individual but others will be larger to accommodate a number of staff performing various duties.

So, typically, we will have several individual partitioned spaces for executives, laboratory managers, administration managers, meeting rooms, staff lunch rooms, shower/change rooms and toilets. There will be small laboratory spaces requiring partitions for environmental control, prevention of contamination, sound-proofing or other reasons. Then there will be the larger laboratory spaces which are open-planned. Finally there will be all the support spaces such as cold rooms, store rooms, glassware wash-up and others.

The individual offices will be the easiest to define in the brief because the floor space allocation for offices is well established. The other individual spaces such as cold rooms, store rooms, etc. are also easy to define but the laboratories, both individual and open-planned, are the areas requiring the most work for both laboratory staff and laboratory designer.

Over the years I have developed a design technique, which will be described in Chapter 2 – Design methodology. This technique has proved itself on numerous commissions, so I commend it to you for your consideration.

The brief for the laboratory spaces should be defined as follows. List all laboratory functions in a Schedule of Accommodation (Figure 1.6). Under each functional space list the equipment on the left hand side of the page. Opposite each item, indicate the length of bench or floor space required for each item, including any associated bench space required. In other words, if an item is 0.6 metres across the front and you need 0.5 metres on the left for, say, a samples tray and 0.7 metres on the right for, say, write-up purposes the length of bench is shown as 1.8 metres.

When you are listing each item of equipment, state the services you will require for that equipment, such as AC power, natural gas, nitrogen, etc., and the type of gas outlet. The two types are quick-connect and push-on hose fitting. The latter is only suitable for low pressure and vacuum.

If the bench-mounted or floor-standing equipment is deeper than, say, 600 mm you will need to mention this on the list.

Later, in Chapter 2, I will explain how your bench lengths are used to calculate the floor area requirement for each laboratory.

SCHEDULE OF ACCOMMODATION
LABORATORY FUNCTION DESCRIPTION
Staff number

Equipment or Function	Equipment Dimensions	Associated bench	Services
Item	length depth height	length	water/waste gases power data
Function	length		

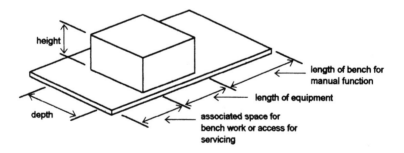

Figure 1.6 Schedule of accommodation showing the method of measuring laboratory equipment and the associated extra bench space

1.7 Storage

Storage is often poorly considered, even forgotten. To avoid benches being used for storage your storage requirements need to be detailed carefully in your brief. It is absolutely critical to have adequate provision for storage of hazardous substances, equipment, and consumables to ensure good housekeeping and therefore safe laboratory operations.

Consider how you receive your chemicals, glassware, plasticware and paper. You may need a receiving area for unpacking if you do not have supplies delivered directly to their destination. Some users like to store supplies in the original packaging to save decanting or to make re-ordering easier. In that case your shelving requirement is likely to be open, widely spaced and deep to accommodate the large packages. If, on the other hand, you break open the packaging and distribute the contents onto shelves or drawers, you need to specify the sizes to fit the size of the articles. For safety and good ergonomics I always recommend narrow shelves to avoid stacking bottles behind each other and always full height cupboards to avoid bending down and reaching into deep under-bench cupboards. Ergonomically, drawers under workbenches provide easier access than cupboards. So if you decide to specify drawers, make sure you also specify the clear height within the drawers to accommodate your requirements.

With the increasing use of equipment and instrumentation on benches, storing reagents on shelves behind benches is to be avoided. If in chemical and pathology laboratories there is a requirement for shelves adjacent to manual work, be sure to specify that you require the reagent shelves to be movable. If the workbench changes from a manual area to a location for large instrumentation such as auto analysers, the reagent shelf can be lifted off to provide more depth on the bench.

As with workbench requirements, your storage requirements should be expressed in terms of shelf length in metres and drawer sizes. Your brief should subdivide your requirements also into open shelves, closed shelves, closed with glass doors, open in separate store room and specify locations for each storage requirement.

Later, in Chapter 2, I will explain how the designer can take your requirements and calculate the floor space requirements of your storage.

1.8 Equipment

For purposes of writing the design brief, the category of equipment can include all floor-mounted items which are not workbenches or storage cupboards. These items are generally refrigerators, freezer cabinets, incubators, ovens, centrifuges, mixers, and now, increasingly, large auto-analysers and other combined instrumentation.

When listing your laboratory equipment, the size of the equipment in the brief should include the clearance space required for servicing which is recommended by the supplier. The laboratory designer may not be familiar with some of your equipment and all the relevant information should be supplied in the brief.

1.9 Work environment

Probably more important than for any other work area, the laboratory has special environmental requirements which need to be carefully considered at the design brief stage.

The high costs associated with providing the ideal environment can be reduced if there is a passive energy building design philosophy. Your brief, however, is not going to provide the design solution but you should express your views on the subject.

The brief should list your requirements in terms of temperature and variation limits, humidity control and, most important, the percentage of recirculated air. Some laboratories cannot tolerate any recirculated air and require 100% fresh air. Your requirements for temperature and humidity will be relatively easy to accommodate but if you require 100% fresh air, because you cannot tolerate air returning to the laboratory through the system, this will add greatly to the project costs and should be carefully considered. The reasons for not recirculating air are generally to avoid accumulating hazardous airborne contaminants or to avoid cross-contamination.

You may also have hot and cold rooms, in which case you will specify the temperature and humidity ranges required.

The mechanical engineering consultant designing your ventilation systems will have to calculate the total heat load generated by the laboratory equipment. The heat load is available from the supplier of the equipment.

Another important factor affecting the design of the air conditioning is the quantity, type and estimated frequency of use of fume cupboards. If the fume cupboard manufacturer is selected during the preparation of the design brief, the mechanical engineer consultant will be given the best information to work on. In selecting the manufacturer you should consider quality, performance, energy saving and compliance with the fume cupboard standards.

1.10 Staff facilities

Unlike other work environments the laboratory is a potentially hazardous area, but in a well-managed and well-designed facility hazards can be kept under control.

Regulations and standards for occupational health and safety cover the laboratory work place quite thoroughly and the design team will necessarily have to be conversant with all the requirements for both the work place and facilities. A professional OH & S consultant should be part of the design team (see 2.1 – Project team).

The design brief will need to include the staff rooms and equipment required for your particular laboratory size, type and staffing. This will include a first-aid room, lunch room with drinking water, locker room and toilets with showers.

Access for the disabled needs to be addressed in the brief. If you express a preference for a single storey laboratory the provision of access for disabled staff and visitors will of course be easy to facilitate. If, however, the building needs to be multi-storied the problem of egress by the disabled escaping from a fire on an upper storey can be solved but with great difficulty.

1.11 Meeting rooms

The last but by no means the least important functional space requirement in the laboratory design brief are the meeting rooms.

Depending on the type and size of the laboratory building, and on the particular needs, there may be a requirement for small meeting rooms, medium size conference rooms and a seminar auditorium.

An example is a research organisation which has 200 staff. They are satisfied with their variety of meeting rooms which are three small meeting rooms to seat 8–10, a conference facility to seat 40 with an operable partition and a sloping floor auditorium to seat all staff.

Meeting rooms need to be sound-proof and this requirement can only be achieved in divisible conference facilities with the best operable walls to an acoustic consultant's specifications.

Facilities for teleconferences may be required in the small meeting rooms and electronic whiteboards are useful for recording proceedings.

Overhead projectors may be appropriate for the conference rooms which should have a level floor allowing various seating configurations.

In the auditorium, film projection and TV monitors have been replaced by computer and video projectors which produce bright, clear definition images displayed on large screens at the front visible from the rear seats. Video cameras with zoom lenses in booths at the rear can record proceedings for transmission to other sites but mainly for the laboratory's own resource collection.

Toilets need to be adjacent to the auditorium to avoid visitors searching for them through the building.

Essential for the proper function of participant interaction is an adjacent space, adequate in size to accommodate the auditorium capacity standing in small groups for discussion and light refreshments. Noticeboards to display the seminar programme and information should be located away from external and auditorium doors. Direct entry for visitors separate to the building entry may be desirable particularly if the facilities are let out to the community at large.

As laboratories are a smoke-free environment, you will have to comply with the law in your country or state regarding provision of smokers' facilities.

1.12 Car parking

The design brief should include the space required for staff car parking and selection of covered or open space. Car parking for visitors should also be included.

Some laboratories have couriers delivering specimens/samples for testing and their access to the laboratory is an important part of the workflow.

In any event, check with the local building authority for their car parking regulations.

1.13 Visitors

Some laboratories encourage visitors to inspect their operation as part of their public relations programme. Others exclude all visitors except those who are involved in their operation, such as trade representatives and service personnel. You will need to consider and specify the access, waiting space, reporting-in and visitor toilets in your design brief.

1.14 Security

As laboratories are a hazardous work environment the staff know the risks and follow the proper safety behaviour. However visitors, particularly intruders, are not aware of the hazards and are a danger to themselves and to the laboratory.

Security has to be considered as one of the most important design problems. The solution can generally be designed into the scheme but it does deserve respect.

The design solution which is a simple physical barrier with the minimum of entry/exit points is generally better than relying on complicated human behaviour and electronic wizardry. It needs to form part of the design brief or will be difficult to achieve later.

Chapter 2

Design methodology

2.1 Project team

The professional team to be assembled for a laboratory building should be selected from consulting architects, designers, engineers and quantity surveyors who have had recent experience and developed expertise in the design and construction of laboratory buildings.

Most major firms will claim to have had relevant experience but laboratories are not like other industrial or academic buildings and require very considerable recent experience in the field. Insist on having the names of the individual professionals who are nominated to work on the project. The individuals who were responsible for the nominated previous experience may no longer be with the firm. They should all have a proven track record and should preferably have worked together before on laboratory projects, as laboratory design requires very close cooperation within the project design team. The client should inspect the completed laboratory buildings nominated by the prospective professionals before selecting the team.

A specialist laboratory designer should be part of the professional team together with an Occupational Health (or Hygiene) and Safety Specialist. The latter would preferably be a member of the client staff and familiar with the hazards but needs to be effective, which is not always possible being in-house.

2.2 Project meetings

At the first project meeting the project design team will be introduced to the client representatives. It is very important to establish right from the outset the lines of communication. As soon as the client has completed the brief, having covered at least all items in Chapter 1 – Design brief, copies should be distributed to all design consultants. Questions on the brief will come quickly as the project design team will want to have a clear understanding of the client requirements.

The laboratory staff responsible for the brief should use lay terms if possible but technical terms may sometimes be unavoidable and may need clarification.

The first meeting should determine the frequency of project meetings, usually weekly and the day of the week which suits everybody. The first few meetings will probably be the most important and should be attended by all. Later, when a pattern is established and members become more interactive outside meetings, the main players may be the only permanent members.

The importance of minuting the decisions of each meeting, corrected at following meetings if necessary, with an 'action' column cannot be overemphasised. There has never been a brief prepared which has not been amended and expanded. New members to the committee need to be informed of decisions made prior to their joining the team.

It is helpful to the project design team to 'illustrate' the descriptions in the brief of laboratory functions and laboratory equipment by touring the client's existing laboratory. It will be an opportunity to explain the deficiencies and inadequacies of the present facility and why indeed they have to refit or build a new laboratory building.

It is sometimes appropriate for the meeting to adjourn to other laboratory buildings, both well established and recently completed, to illustrate good design or to show what not to do.

2.3 Project programme and budget

The design brief should only describe the laboratory users' requirements. If the client has target dates and funding limits the client should issue a separate document to instruct the project design team on the design and construction programme and the project budget.

2.4 Returning the brief

After completing their analysis of the brief, target dates and budget, the design team should 'return' the brief to the client with their recommendations as specialist consultants, for which they were employed. The client will agree with some of their recommendations, not with others, and the brief is amended accordingly.

The architect's submission generally takes the form of function/room data sheets in the design team's own format, without changing user requirements. The term 'needs analysis' is sometimes used for this format. At this time, it may be appropriate for the design team to take the client to completed laboratories to illustrate their recommendations.

2.5 Design synthesis

Having analysed the design brief, the specialist laboratory design consultant will commence the process of assimilation and synthesis. My design philosophy has always been to develop the building design from the interior, the work place.

The various functional spaces are assembled in the relationships shown by the client's Space Relationship Diagram or 'Bubble Diagram' (Figure 1.2). The floor area in square metres for each functional space is estimated at this stage by multiplying the length of workbenches and floor-standing equipment by a factor of 1.75. If, however, you want to allow for unforeseen and future requirements, and if the budget allows, multiply by a factor of up to 2.00. The length of workbenches and floorstanding equipment is shown in the Client's Schedule (Figure 1.6). At the same time, one has to keep in mind several other considerations, not least of which are the building regulations, codes of practice and standards of your country.

The design synthesis is a very complex process of amalgamating all the many parts of the laboratory into a whole. The conception may produce more than one design solution and these alternative designs need to be tested against all the user requirements until a preferred scheme is selected.

This stage is called the scheme plan and an example is illustrated in Figure 2.1. At this stage we are looking only at the 'big picture'. Only the main laboratory areas are shown, with the general circulation corridors and the internal laboratory circulation as illustrated in Figure 2.2. This diagram will of course reflect the building regulation requirements in terms of fire egress.

2.6 Design development

Having all agreed on the scheme plan, the design is then developed in more detail particularly with regard to the laboratory workbenches and laboratory services infrastructure as illustrated in Figure 2.3. It is important for the developed design to be complete in all detailed requirements and agreed as the 'final' design before the 'client approved' plans are passed on to the architects' contract documentation team. Their responsibility is to take the design drawings and turn them into another form of drawings called 'building contract documentation' which can be readily understood by those who will prepare a tender price and later have sufficient information to use for construction purposes. The contract documentation team will want all design decisions to have been made or their work is delayed by questions and answers.

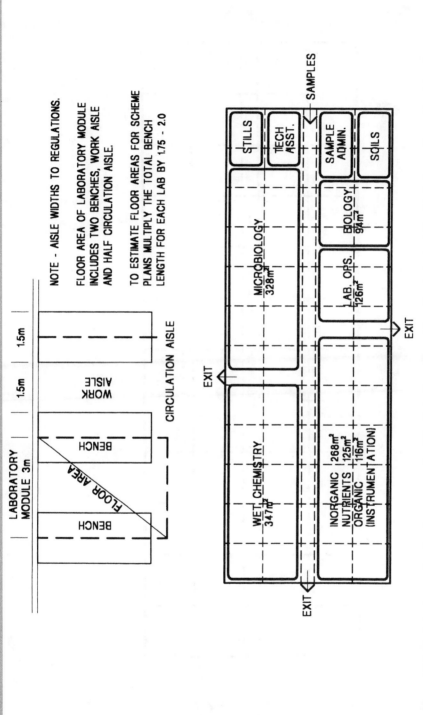

Figure 2.1 Typical scheme plan showing an example of the first attempt to achieve the desired relationship between the various laboratory spaces

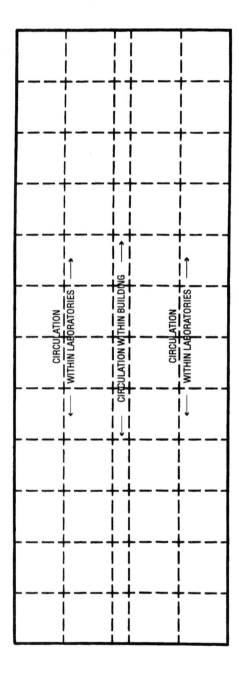

Figure 2.2 Typical building circulation diagram showing an example of the single corridor plan and explaining the circulation system. Alternative corridor/circulation designs are discussed under 3.4 – Interior designs

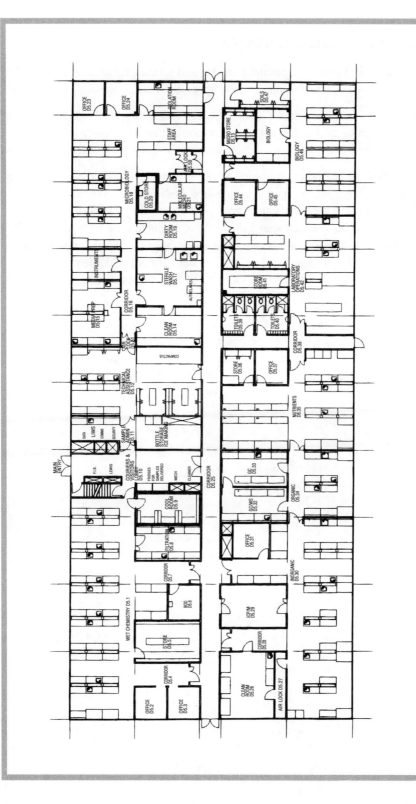

Figure 2.3 Typical developed laboratory floor plan showing the final layout of the example in Figures 2.1 and 2.2

2.7 Contract documentation

The building contract between laboratory owner and building contractor will include the agreement, the contract drawings and the specification.

The agreement can take many forms, none of which is the subject of my design guide. The same can be said of the specification except that I will mention a number of design recommendations in later chapters which will form part of the specification.

I recommend that the laboratory furniture including benches, workstations, balance benches, equipment frames, storage cupboards and shelves should be manufactured and installed by a joinery subcontractor specialising in laboratory furniture. The subcontractor should be selected after the client has inspected the work of available specialist joiners and obtained designs and quotations from each firm. The selected firm is nominated and their quotation included in the contract documents as a 'provisional sum' to be allowed by the main contractor in their tender.

I also recommend that essential equipment, such as fume cupboards which are so important to the proper function of the laboratory, should be selected from the available products for their performance and suiting the client's requirements rather than the lowest tender. The selected manufacturer can be nominated in the tender documents with a provisional sum equivalent to the quotation with a 2 year service agreement.

Chapter 3

Site and buildings

3.1 Location

Laboratories are classified by the local planning authority in their zoning of the different land uses.

Having selected a particular district it is essential to visit the local planning authority to inspect the zoning plan to determine the areas in that district which have been allocated for the laboratory classification.

Referring to 1.5 – Hazards, it is necessary to discuss the laboratory effluents (liquid, airborne, etc.) described in the brief with the relevant local authorities to check if they have any objections and to receive their instructions for installation of control strategies such as dilution pits and airborne contaminant extraction locations.

At the same time, the design team should obtain copies of the local planning and building regulations, which may have special conditions in addition to the country or state building code and regulations.

It is best to get the neighbours on your side by relieving their anxiety at the prospect of having a laboratory in the immediate vicinity. Better that they learn the facts from you and your concerns for them than from the media.

3.2 Site planning

Before commencing site planning it is necessary to obtain copies of all relevant regulations governing the location of dangerous or hazardous stores including laboratory gas cylinders and the access for vehicles. These regulations have considerable implications on planning.

If the laboratory is not a stand-alone building but is associated with other buildings such as manufacturing, warehousing, administration, engineering, staff cafeteria/amenities and public access showroom, there are building regulations governing the physical separation of the laboratory from all other buildings. This separation can take the form of either a fire-rated isolation wall construction or a given distance of open space between the buildings.

Other considerations in site planning will be posed by matters of security and vehicular access which are both better controlled with physical planning than elaborate electronic devices subject to control of staff behaviour and accidental human error. Vehicular access is normally restricted to deliveries of laboratory supplies and samples or specimens for testing.

From the outside any confusion by visitors can be reduced if the visitors' entrance is obvious and clearly signposted. This eliminates the possibility of visitors wandering around the site and makes unauthorised visitors more conspicuous.

The site plan should be as simple, orderly and regular as possible. It should allow for expansion of the laboratory as an extension of the plan and avoid having to turn into an L-shape, or worse, a separate building. An L-shape extension generally produces confusion at the junction where the linear planning turns the corner. A separate building is not easy to access but can be successful if it is a separate laboratory function.

3.3 Building design

My design philosophy is based on looking at the various work places first and systematically building up a picture of the whole work environment – the building. I avoid having any pre-conceived images of the building. I was once asked at the first briefing session at a university, 'what will the building look like?'. I just had to admit that I had no idea at all, but quickly explained why I had to go through the design process before any images would start to emerge.

Laboratory work calls for controlled environmental conditions. These conditions can be provided by expensive, energised, high-tech equipment or by what is known as passive energy design. The former solves problems created by building designs which are conceived without regard to conservation of energy and the latter, which is fortunately becoming mandatory by some clients and the design philosophy of most architects and mechanical engineers, uses to advantage solar energy and energy generated by the laboratory equipment and occupants.

The architects' role in energy conservation is mainly in the orientation of the building to expose the minimum wall area to solar energy, to use indirect natural sunlight where possible, in, say, non-laboratory spaces, and to design the wall and roof fabric of the building to insulate heat exchange from outside to inside and in reverse, depending on climatic conditions.

Direct sunlight onto benches should be avoided as some chemicals can become unstable if exposed for an extended period. Some instruments cannot tolerate direct sunlight.

As the design team leader, the architect can encourage the engineering consultants to follow an energy conservation policy including the selection of low-brightness reflector type light fittings, power supply and air-conditioning systems coordinated with local and general exhaust ventilation.

Standards recommend levels of illumination at bench level, quality of power supply, quality of laboratory gases, room temperature variation and humidity controls and these recommendations should be followed even if they are not mandatory. More and more standards are becoming mandatory and most clients are adopting these standards as company policy.

Figure 3.1 shows a cross-section through a laboratory building which has many desirable features. Firstly, the laboratory is on one level allowing maximum flexibility in rearrangement of departments, level transport of chemicals, glassware and other supplies on trolleys and staff convenience generally. Secondly, the laboratory water, waste, gas and power services can be reticulated in the accessible sub-floor area and supplied to the benches through the floor. Thirdly, the roof space directly over the laboratory can accommodate the air-conditioning equipment and ducts, local exhaust fans and ducts. The ceiling height should be selected to suit the laboratory function and may very well be determined by building regulations. Opinion varies on floor-to-ceiling heights but the lower height, if suitable for the laboratory function, has energy conservation advantages in the reduced volume of conditioned air and electrical power needed for illumination.

If it is not possible to have a single-storey laboratory one of the disadvantages of a multi-storied building is the need for vertical service ducts. Vertical service ducts have in the past contributed to the spread of fire through multi-storied laboratory buildings, so regulations are likely to require these ducts to have fire-rated enclosures. The horizontal reticulated gas services from the vertical ducts to the laboratory benches at each floor should not be covered. If enclosed, gas leaks can build up within the confined space and create an explosion hazard. Standards or regulations require such ducts to be ventilated. If the gas lines are fixed neatly to the wall, they should not be considered an eyesore but a design for easy maintenance and identification if location is needed in a hurry.

Other disadvantages of a multi-storied building are the need for goods lifts for the safe transportation of flammable liquids, laboratory wastes, bulky stores, and heavy laboratory equipment. Fire-isolated stairs for safe egress of staff escaping from a fire and smoke are an additional cost to multi-storied buildings.

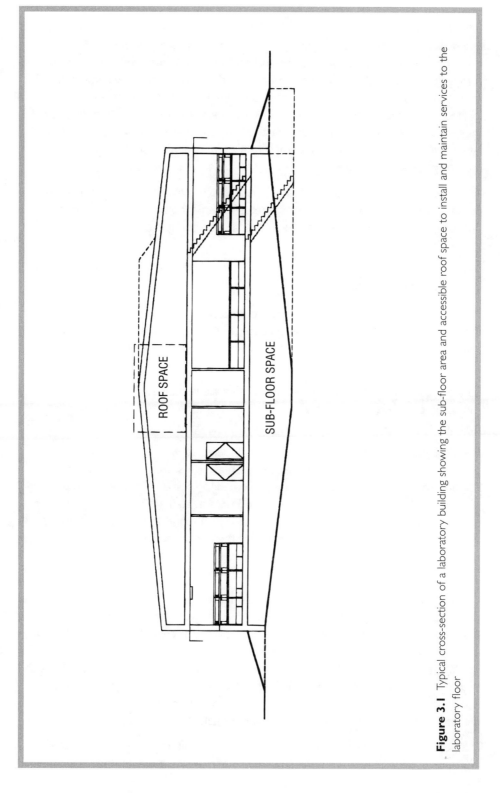

Figure 3.1 Typical cross-section of a laboratory building showing the sub-floor area and accessible roof space to install and maintain services to the laboratory floor

The laboratory floor should not be graded to floor wastes but should be level to provide a level surface for movable workbenches, under-bench storage cupboards and drawers, and floor-standing equipment. If there is a risk of water overflowing onto the floor from sinks, water baths and equipment it is more effective to install gratings at the door than have a floor waste. Exceptions to the above would be animal rooms and laboratories requiring to be washed, when the wastes should be located in a corner furthest from the door. Laboratories are not washed down as they used to be before the current practice of using smaller volumes of liquids with fewer spills. Floor wastes are sometimes installed under safety showers, but for the reasons given in 3.4 – Interior design this has some disadvantages.

To achieve a clear rectangular laboratory floor space the structural columns should not impinge on the laboratory floor space, so external columns should project outwards and internal columns project into the corridor space.

3.4 Interior design

The trend in architecture to irregular, sometimes curved-shaped, spaces, away from the modernist square or rectangular spaces is not suitable for laboratory spaces. Laboratory benches and equipment are rectangular and do not fit into irregular shapes.

So the most suitable floor plans for laboratories are rectangular. Two alternative plans should be considered. One has a central corridor and the other has two parallel corridors.

The dual corridor plan (Figure 3.2) is generally selected when there are a large proportion of laboratory support facilities such as bulk store rooms, cool rooms, isolation rooms, dark rooms, special instrumentation rooms, autoclave washing facilities, etc. These areas, which can be windowless as staff are not working in there constantly, can be successfully arranged in the central 'core', as it is known, between the two corridors. The staff workbenches are then arranged between the two corridors and window walls. A disadvantage of this arrangement is that access to the facilities from the laboratories is across the corridor.

The single corridor plan Figure 3.3 is generally favoured, however, as it is more flexible. The areas on both sides should be the same width for maximum flexibility, so the single corridor should be central. In the past, a plan with central structural columns and an off-set corridor was popular, but with the trend towards more open combined laboratory areas, the unequal widths became restrictive in the allocation and reallocation of spaces. The laboratory support facilities in this plan can be arranged immediately adjacent to the laboratory they serve. If the building shape is irregular, one can still design the plan with the basic principles of the single or dual corridor plans.

In at least two instances, to my certain knowledge, architects have designed new laboratory buildings with a central corridor wide enough to accommodate

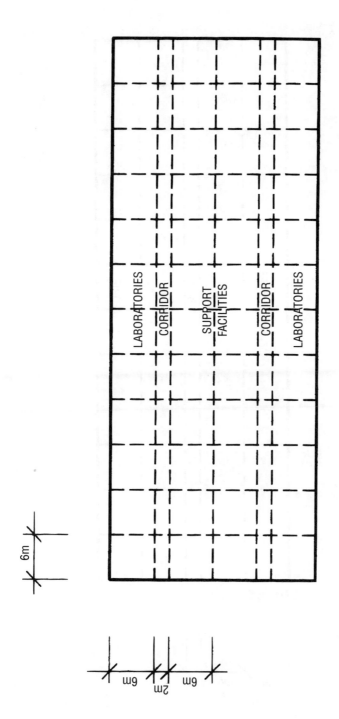

Figure 3.2 Dual corridor plan showing the two parallel corridors serving the laboratory spaces along the window walls and the support spaces between the corridors

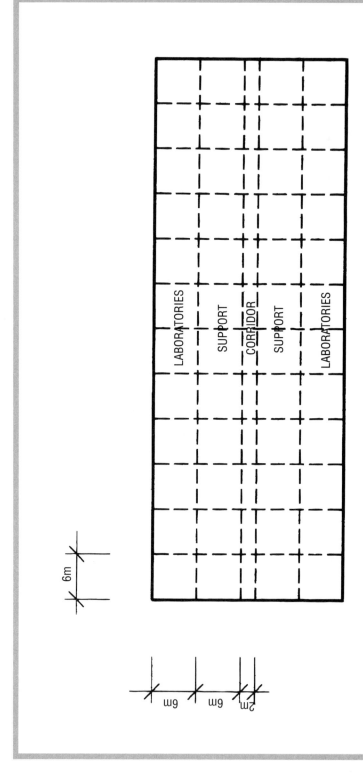

LABORATORIES

SUPPORT

CORRIDOR

SUPPORT

LABORATORIES

6m

6m 6m 2m

Figure 3.3 Single corridor plan showing the laboratory space on both sides of a single corridor

refrigerators! In both cases they claimed to have come to the conclusion that this design was desirable because they had seen wide corridors full of refrigerators and other laboratory equipment during their 'research'. I was able to explain to the architect that the equipment was only in the corridor because the laboratories were fitted out with fixed benching with no space for floor-standing equipment, so they had no choice but to put the equipment in the corridor.

The need for space in laboratories for equipment is mentioned under 4.1 – Workbenches. The width of the main central corridor should conform to the building regulations but should not be less than 1500 mm. If it is much wider, there is a temptation to place objects in the corridor and even if they are only temporary they can be an obstruction to the required fire egress width. Corridors should be clear for rapid egress so obstructions of any kind should be avoided. Doors opening into corridors should be recessed.

A good rule in laboratory interior design is to arrange the workbenches at right angles to the window walls. This arrangement creates quiet work 'bays' free from through-traffic. Also, working at the benches one is neither casting a shadow on the bench nor looking up into the glare from the window. The workbenches can be fitted to the window wall or can be separated from the window wall by a walk aisle. I adopt the latter plan for high risk laboratories such as oils laboratories, where there is a higher risk of fire and an alternative escape is provided by the aisle at the window.

The workbenches at right angles to the window walls are called 'peninsula benches', and when separated from the wall are called 'island benches'. If you are considering island benches you have to realise that services will have to come up through the floor or down from the ceiling. Drainage from island benches has to go down through the floor, unless you adopt a pump-out or vacuum extraction system up through the ceiling. Peninsula benches can be serviced from the wall to which they are attached.

I try to avoid planning benches against partitions. Facing the wall the worker will not see what is happening in the laboratory, which may be dangerous and the worker is preventing supervision of the bench work. Also the worker may not realise that fellow workers have left the laboratory, and is working in isolation which is not recommended.

Under 1.4 – Staff, I describe the three options for the relationship of staff write-up space to benchwork space. Option C is preferred by OH & S professionals with option B their second choice. However, I have found the allocation of bench space to the various functions is most popular with staff if the write-up desk is close to the window, next to the individual's bench space and equipment with the wet area, if any, at the other end next to the circulation aisle. A screen can be installed between the write-up desk and the workbench.

Regulations and standards control the minimum widths of work aisles, circulation aisles and other spaces. See Figure 2.1.

For maximum flexibility laboratory functions should be combined into shared open spaces. However, some functions cannot be shared. Those which need separation due to the nature of the hazard, e.g. ionising radiation, carcinogens; the need for speech privacy, e.g. supervisor's office; to minimise disruption, e.g. centrifuge noise, or need special environmental conditions. Obviously most of the laboratory support facilities mentioned above will be partitioned. If laboratory work areas are partitioned for each department, when any one department expands or contracts it is either cramped or wasteful of space. Open planning allows departments to be reallocated space without demolishing partitions.

Plan for storage space, preferably adjacent to the main circulation for easy access by staff replenishing supplies. Too often storage is an afterthought or at best very inadequate and one of the chief failings of a design.

Laboratory work requires a higher level of illumination at the workbench, generally 500 lux, and to conserve energy it is best to have light coloured walls, ceiling, floor and furniture surfaces. Prismatic diffusers under fluorescent tube fittings should be avoided as they create 'reflective glare' on the bench surface. To make the best use of available light sources, high efficiency luminaires with mirror louvres, electronic ballasts and automatic dimming with daylight sensors can provide energy savings of up to 75%.

Wall and ceiling surfaces should be impermeable, non-porous and smooth for easy cleaning.

Laboratory floors should be level. If there is a particular requirement to wash down the floor as in, for example, an autopsy laboratory, floor waste gully traps will have to be installed. If the floor is not washed down regularly, the water trap may evaporate exposing the laboratory environment to the contaminated air in the drains. This situation can be prevented by filling the gully from an adjacent water fixture which is being used regularly.

Floor coverings should be pre-finished sheet vinyl or equivalent material manufactured specifically for the laboratory use with welded joins, taken 150 mm up the walls. Abrasive-surfaced materials should not be used as they will collect dirt from shoes and are difficult to clean. Laboratories are not the wet areas they used to be, with good management insisting on spills being dried as soon as they occur. However, some laboratories such as for autopsy are washed down and need non-slip floors.

If there is a risk of flooding from water baths, wash-up sinks, etc. floor wastes will not prevent the water escaping as floors have to be level and not graded to floor wastes. However, grates can be provided at the laboratory door openings.

Laboratories should include the provision of a safety station consolidating all equipment for fire fighting and accidents at regulation maximum travel distance from any point on the laboratory floor. This facility would include the safety shower, face and eye wash so that the user has a choice. Laboratories with large amounts of corrosive material should have drench shower enclosures. The safety station should not be installed outside the laboratory, for example in the corridor, as the laboratory door is an obstruction to easy immediate access. The shower should not be located in a recess which might become a convenient space for storage but at a point which forms part of the essential circulation, such as the aisle near the laboratory entry door. Architects often provide floor wastes under safety showers, but this can lead to the water in the floor waste trap evaporating, exposing the drain and polluting the laboratory atmosphere. Instead of a floor waste one can test the safety shower by holding a bucket under the shower head.

3.5 Special laboratories

Laboratories used for special functions, defined in the design brief as radioactive, pathogenic, tissue culture, animal, etc., cannot be accommodated in the multi-purpose general laboratory spaces described above but must be purpose built.

The design brief for these laboratories should be prepared by OH & S specialists, e.g. radiation safety officer and microbiological serving officer, but still may not be complete in terms of all the client's requirements and may not include all the regulations of the authorities having jurisdiction over the particular specialised laboratory function.

It will therefore be of paramount importance that all the contractors responsible for the installation of the special laboratory are aware of all the planning and construction requirements. These requirements are subject to change and the current regulations should be obtained and held on site for reference.

The special laboratories are best located in the 'support' facilities space in Figure 3.4, so that they do not interrupt the large continuous ribbon of general laboratory space at the perimeter of the building. A common mistake by architects is to provide only standard doors to these rooms when a much larger access is required for large equipment such as an electron microscope, large autoclave, etc.

Access to these laboratories is, in cases such as animal laboratories, an important planning study and needs careful coordination.

3.6 External bulk storage

If bulk storage facilities for hazardous substances are sited at a convenient distance from the laboratory building with all-weather covered concrete path access, suitable for trolleys and carts, without stairs, staff can be encouraged, if not instructed, to keep only small quantities of hazardous substances such as flammable, corrosive and poisons in the laboratories.

Unless small containers are purchased, safe decanting benches with effective local exhaust ventilation and designed with ergonomic criteria will be required at the main storage location. The same OH & S criteria apply to the facilities for delivery to the bulk storage by road transport. All bulk storage facilities have to be designed to the regulations of the authorities having jurisdiction over the hazardous substances. Documentation of designs have to be submitted to the authorities for approval before construction and inspected by authority representatives and approved before occupation.

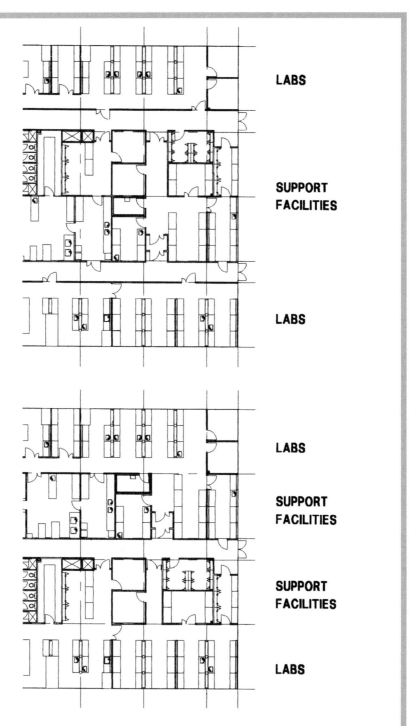

LABS

SUPPORT FACILITIES

LABS

LABS

SUPPORT FACILITIES

SUPPORT FACILITIES

LABS

Figure 3.4 Laboratory support facilities in dual and single corridor plans showing the closer relationship of laboratory spaces to support spaces in the single corridor plan

Chapter 4

Laboratory furniture and services

4.1 Workbenches

The brief to the design team should describe the function of each laboratory so that an appropriate bench design can be submitted for their consideration.

Laboratory functions were performed manually on benches in the past. Some tasks are still performed in much the same way but more and more tasks can now be performed more accurately, faster and with greater safety to the operator by equipment that uses modern technology. The scientist has an ever-increasing range of automated, electronic, mechanical and robotic equipment to select for tasks which were previously performed manually.

The effect of the introduction of this new instrumentation into laboratories has been the need to create new designs and arrangements of benches and desks. The new equipment comes in many shapes and sizes. Although most equipment is designed for bench-mounting, some are larger and are floor-standing. Both are having an impact on bench design and the need for benches at all.

As an example, high performance liquid chromatography (HPLC) is a group of analytical and recording instruments which are interconnected and placed either in line or stacked one above the other. If placed on an island or peninsula bench the backs are more accessible than if they were placed against a wall.

If the room plan allows only wall benches, trolley benches for instruments improve access to the rear of instruments for connection and servicing.

Another design solution is to split the peninsula or island bench into two benches with a narrow access aisle between them. This aisle is used only for connecting, disconnecting and servicing the backs of instruments.

Floor-standing equipment requires a radical change in bench design. Traditionally laboratories have been completely fitted with wall benches and peninsula or island benches – no allowance was made for the introduction of floor-standing equipment. When freezer cabinets, larger centrifuges and the like became available and were required, they had to be placed on the only available floor space, the corridor!

The solution to this problem is to install movable benches. If benching is movable, the laboratory can be rearranged to accommodate the floor-standing equipment and other changed requirements. Maximum flexibility can then be achieved. This design solution is illustrated in Figures 4.1 and 4.2 and Plates 1 to 5.

When shelving for reagents and other supplies is required convenient to movable workbenches, the shelving can be supported on 'services bollards' which stand on a services spine. This design is illustrated in Figure 4.3 and mentioned under 4.5 – Laboratory services.

Manual work is, of course, still performed in laboratories and recent technology has improved facilities for manual tasks in terms of the work surface material and the height of the surface. Generally, new surface materials are resistant to chemicals such as acids, dyes and stains as they are impervious and the dried chemical can be rubbed off the surface with an abrasive pad without damage to the 'solid surface' material.

When selecting bench surface materials, the design team should obtain samples of materials from the suppliers. The client can then apply the chemicals and test the stain removal procedure recommended by the suppliers. I believe this is a more direct approach than relying on so-called 'laboratory tests' supplied by manufacturers. Other tests by the client may include heat, impact, cold (liquid nitrogen) and abrasion.

One of the many advantages of movable benches is that the height of the work surface can be adjusted to suit the tasks and the body dimensions of the individual staff using the bench. This can be achieved only with movable benches which can have a mechanically driven or gas-operated bench height adjusting mechanism (Figure 4.4).

The foregoing applies to laboratories with mainly dry processes. Laboratories employing wet processes need continuous fixed workbenches to contain spills, as illustrated in Figure 4.5. Some degree of flexibility can still be achieved by benches being supported on their own metal frame and not on the cupboards and drawer units. The cupboard and drawer units are stand-alone and being movable can be placed anywhere under the benches.

For undergraduate teaching laboratories I recommend a design which will promote a higher use of available resources.

Some university clients are now insisting that the various departments agree on a laboratory design which is practical for teaching all disciplines. If courses offered or student enrolments change, a redistribution of teaching laboratory resources can be made with minimal alterations.

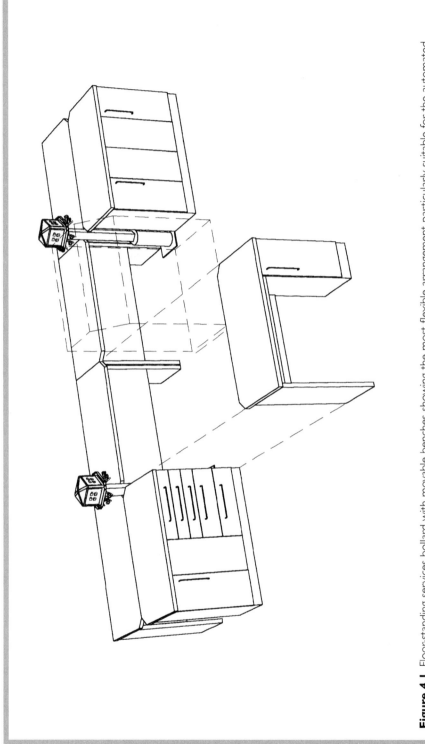

Figure 4.1 Floor-standing services bollard with movable benches showing the most flexible arrangement particularly suitable for the automated laboratory *(continued overleaf)*

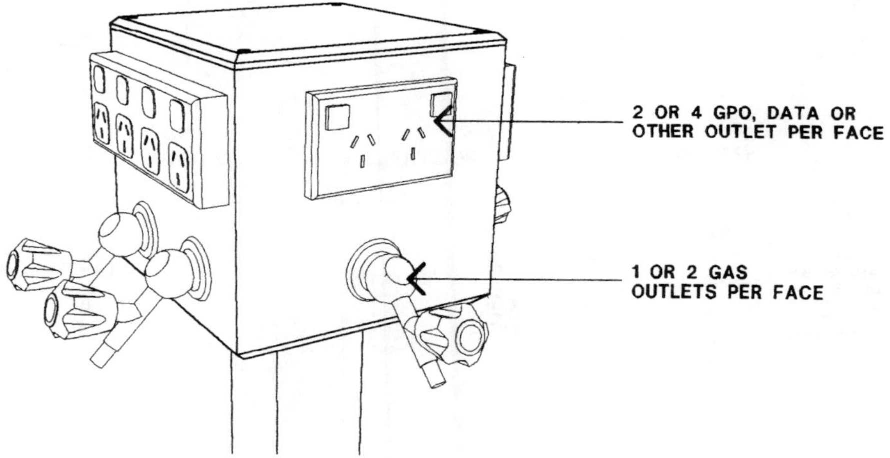

2 OR 4 GPO, DATA OR
OTHER OUTLET PER FACE

1 OR 2 GAS
OUTLETS PER FACE

HEAD DETAIL

Figure 4.1 (Continued)

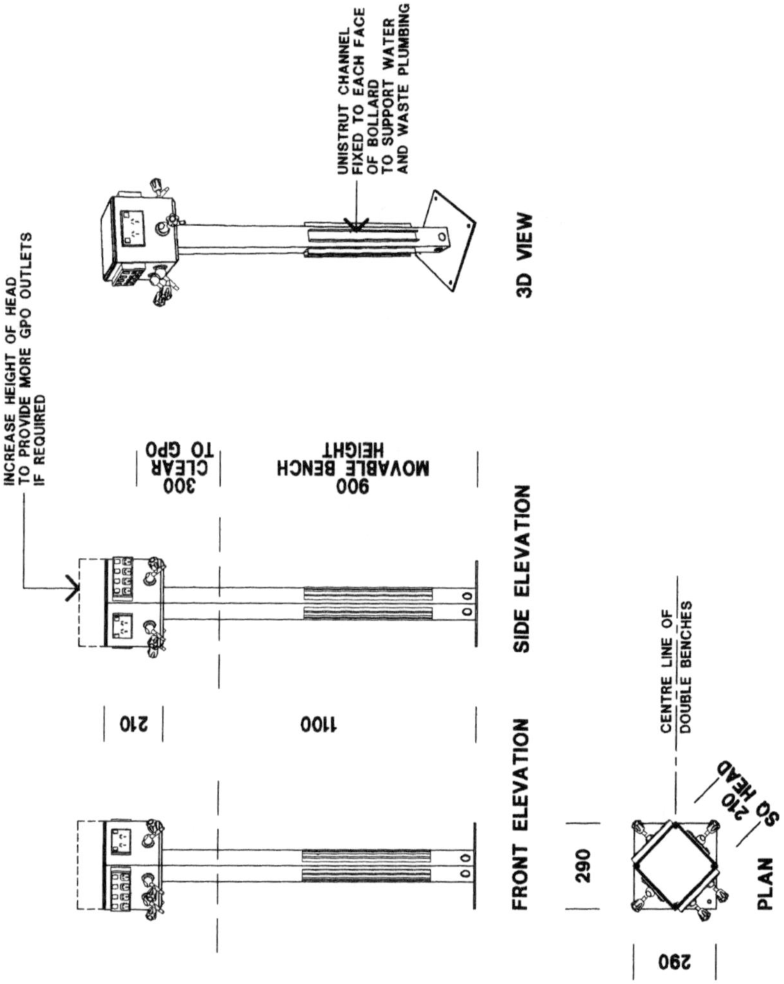

Figure 4.1 (Continued)

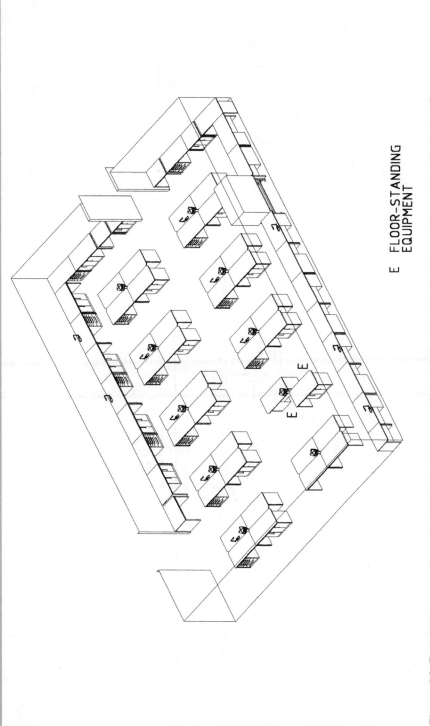

E FLOOR-STANDING EQUIPMENT

Figure 4.2 Typical laboratory with services bollards, equipment and movable benches showing the modular spacing of bollards at 3 metres

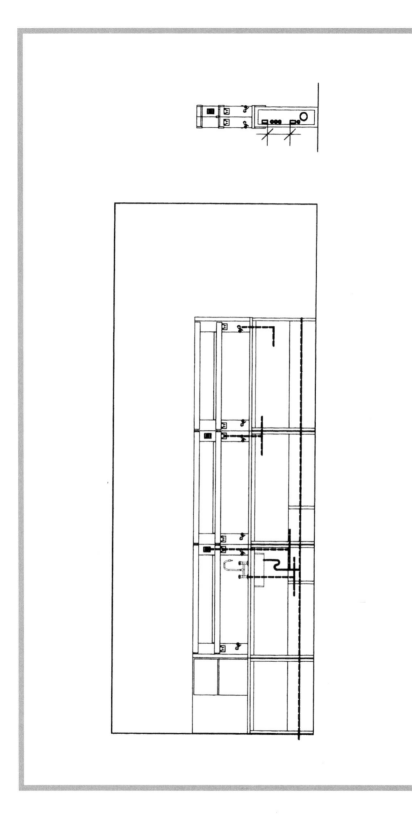

Figure 4.3 Services spine with movable benches and movable over-bench shelves showing the laboratory services on bollards and not on fixed reagent shelves (*continued overleaf*)

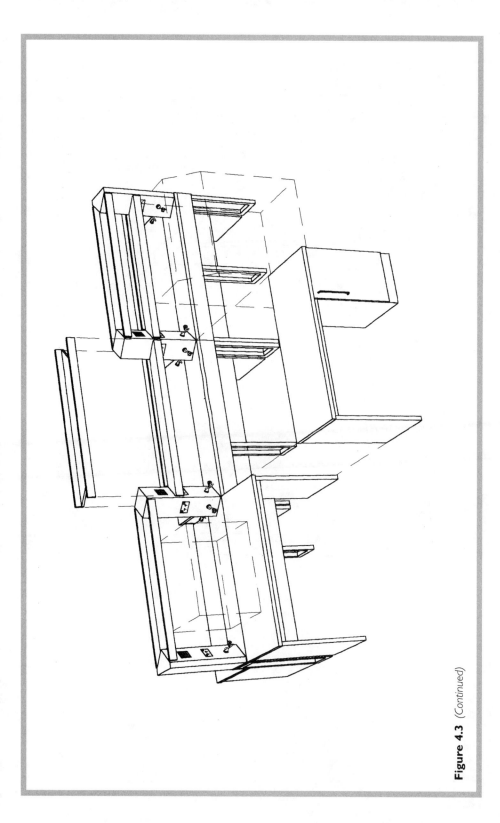

Figure 4.3 (Continued)

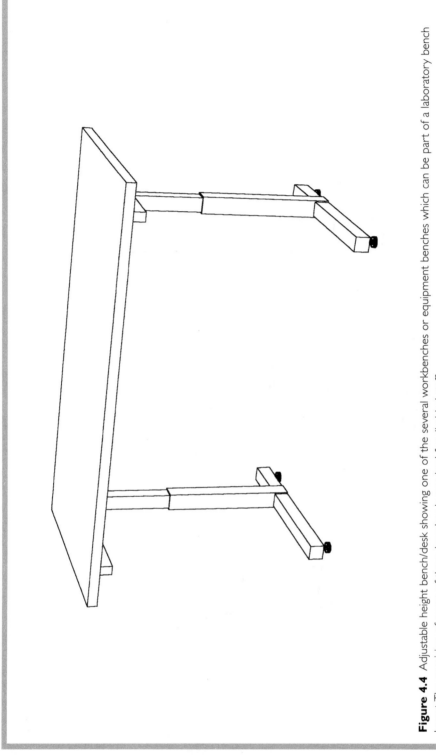

Figure 4.4 Adjustable height bench/desk showing one of the several workbenches or equipment benches which can be part of a laboratory bench layout. The provision of some of these benches is required for disabled staff

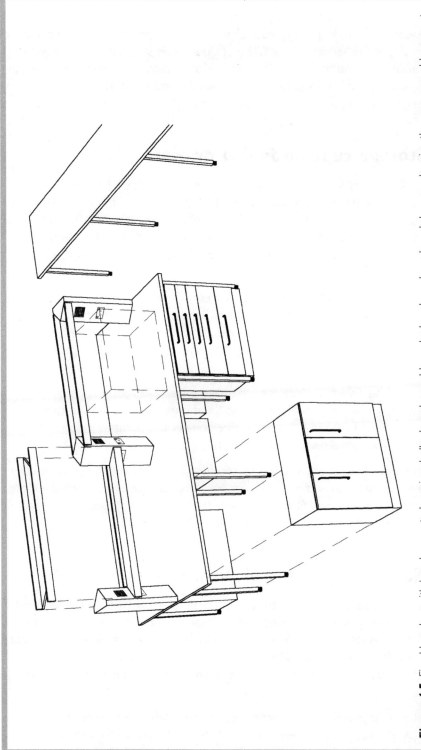

Figure 4.5 Fixed benches with bench-mounted services bollards and movable under-bench cupboards and drawers showing the same movable reagent shelves as in Figure 4.3 with fixed benches for wet laboratories

One of my designs for multi-purpose laboratories is illustrated in Figure 4.6. The Practical Mode shows the movable benches in the traditional arrangement of double-sided benches with students facing each other across the bench which has power and gases available at the 'services bollard'. The Lecture Mode shows the benches, which would now be adjusted to desk height, arranged so that all the students are facing the lecturer. The third plan, Examination Mode shows the desks spaced out sideways for the necessary separation for written examinations.

4.2 Storage cupboards and drawers

Storage of laboratory supplies and small equipment has traditionally been accommodated under the workbench, on shelves at the back of the workbench and in full height glass-fronted wall cabinets. More recently an increase in safety awareness in laboratories has resulted in a reduction in the user requirements for reagent shelving and the quantity of under-bench cupboards in favour of full height wall storage cabinets.

Reaching over and across the instruments on benches for reagents is considered hazardous for both personnel and instruments. Bending down to reach into deep under-bench cupboards is also considered hazardous to the individual and to those passing by. Standing at full height cabinets to access supplies is safer and good ergonomic practice.

Compactus storage might be ideal for office files and supplies but may be hazardous in laboratories. The moving shelf units can spill and break glass chemical bottles and the concentration of chemicals created by the compactus system may violate the standard for maximum allowable volume of chemicals to be stored in the laboratory.

Storage systems which coordinate the main central bulk store with the in-laboratory storage reduce material handling. By storing bulk supplies in drawers which stack into floor delivery carts and then fit into under-bench drawer cabinets, supplies are only handled at the initial delivery and unpacking and sorting into drawer units.

4.3 Non-joinery items of furniture

Apart from the basic benches and storage the design brief will include special items of furniture and equipment described under Chapter 5 – Equipment, such as anti-vibration benches for balances and microscopes. Figure 4.7 shows a design which has a heavy steel frame, 'solid surface' bench top and elastomeric bearings which isolate the bench top from structure-borne vibrations. The size of the bench should be in the brief.

Analytical and other equipment benches need to have adjustable height to suit various shapes and sizes of the equipment. If access is needed to the top of equipment it may have to be lower.

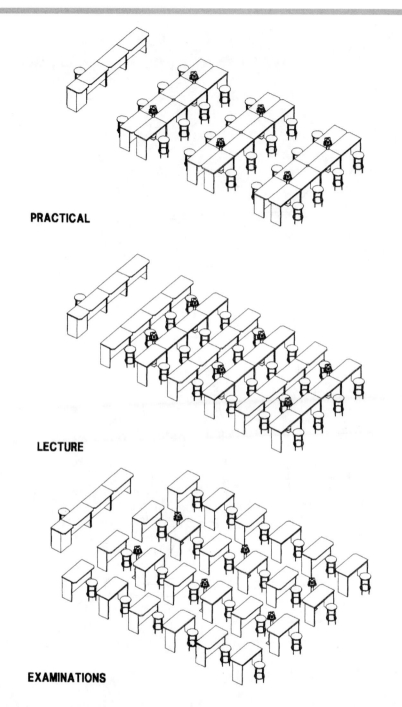

PRACTICAL

LECTURE

EXAMINATIONS

Figure 4.6 Multi-purpose teaching laboratories showing how students' benches can be arranged to suit laboratory practical work, lectures or examinations in laboratories fitted with services bollards and movable benches

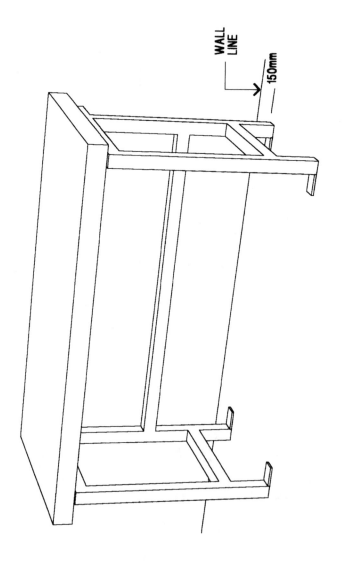

WALL
LINE

150mm

Figure 4.7 Anti-vibration bench showing the frame kept clear of the wall to allow space for service pipes

Fume cupboards are best supported on a metal frame, as illustrated in Figure 4.8 so that access to the underside of the fume cupboard for repairs and cleaning is possible. Although it is convenient to the fume cupboard, flammable liquids should not be stored under the fume cupboard, which is an 'ignition source'.

The space under the fume cupboard is needed by seated operators for good ergonomics.

Flammable liquids storage cabinets should comply with the relevant code or standard and nominated in the brief. Not all cabinets are manufactured with insulation between the inner metal and outer metal linings to protect the flammable liquids from fire.

4.4 Glass wash facilities

In many new laboratories centralised glass washing facilities for the whole laboratory have replaced the old-style large double bowl sinks and drainers at the ends of peninsula benches. Used glassware is collected on trolleys and taken to the mechanical wash machines and autoclaves, which have special trays for laboratory glassware. Small sinks in the laboratory can be used for rinsing prior to placing on the trolley.

This central facility has meant wash sinks no longer take up valuable bench space and avoids the problem of water splashing onto benches. The need for water supply and liquid disposal can still be provided by drip cups or small sinks which take up less space and would be better located closer to the task.

However, if the client has asked for glass washing facilities within the laboratory, a facility should be located with minimum disruption to the workbenches and provide the required sink bowl size and depth, the draining area if needed, wall-mounted drying racks, soap dispensers, hot and cold taps, etc. If the wash-up sinks are to be on the peninsula workbenches try not to locate them on the end, as users will be vulnerable to accidental collision with through-traffic. Sinks in the workbenches are likely to receive concentrated chemicals so their material is more critical than for wash-up sinks. As with the bench top materials samples of sinks for the laboratory should be tested by the client rather than relying on product sales literature.

4.5 Laboratory services

With the introduction of electronic instruments and automated equipment, more power services are required as well as a wide variety of specialty gases. Clean power and power with other special requirements of stability, and various computer, data and telephone requirements are increasing. Standby power is required if instrumentation or other power operations require uninterrupted supply, such as in health care facilities.

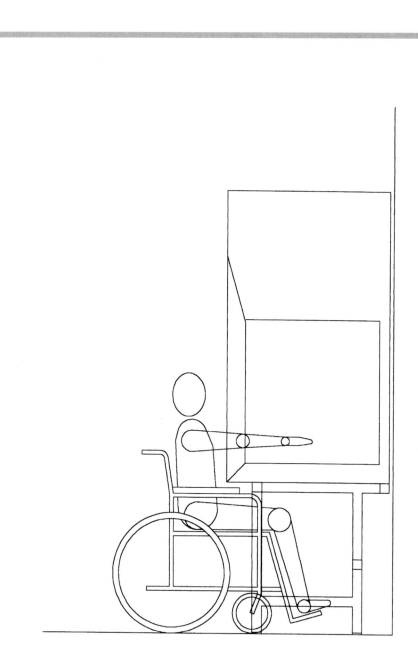

Figure 4.8 Fume cupboard support frame showing the frame kept clear of the wall to allow service pipes and open in front for knee space, access for the disabled and storage cupboards

The old traditional installation of laboratory services to fixed workbenches was to reticulate below bench level with outlets spaced at regular intervals along the back of the bench top. This method has the disadvantage of a services infrastructure which is hard to change. Horizontal reticulation above floor level prevents the rearranging of bench layout.

If, on the other hand, services are reticulated below the laboratory floor and rise at regular intervals on the laboratory grid, aisles and benches can be rearranged to suit changing requirements without interrupting the services infrastructure.

This better option is of course only available in single-storey laboratories, buildings with interstitial service floors and where there is no objection to services in the floor below. I recommend where possible the reticulation of services below the laboratory floor if access to services is available as illustrated in Figure 3.1. In the early 1980s I designed and patented a 'bollard' system, providing laboratory services to movable benches. The bollards provide power, gases, water and drainage for sinks. Spaced at regular intervals of, say, 3 metres in both directions, this grid of bollards provides all laboratory services to movable benches, including sink benches, in any desired layout. The benches can be either in small island formations or in long lines incorporating more than one bollard. Aisles can be planned in either direction and changed if the original layout proves unsatisfactory. Furthermore floor-standing equipment such as freezer cabinets, large centrifuges and robotic analysers can be incorporated into the bench layout. Figure 4.2 and Plates 1 to 5 show some of my completed bollard system laboratories.

In the past laboratory services were incorporated into the reagent shelving. It was all right then, because bench work was performed manually. Now that more and more work is automated, space has to be provided for the instrumentation and sometimes very large machines. The bench depth may not be sufficient to accommodate some machines so the fixed reagent shelving is restrictive. My solution to this design problem is to install services 'bollards' on a services spine as illustrated in Figure 4.3. The reagent shelves no longer have services in them so can be removed if the extra bench depth is required.

The design of services installations is performed by engineering consultants who should have had extensive and recent experience in laboratory buildings. Fire detection and suppression services have to be carefully considered in laboratory buildings. Hence the need for experienced consulting engineers.

Water supply is a service in which the local supply authority take a particular interest to avoid the laboratory contaminating the town water. Isolating the laboratory with a 'break tank' on the roof is one solution. The town water drops into the tank preventing any possible transmission of contaminants. Water gravitates to the laboratories or can be pumped for higher and more reliable pressure. Back flow prevention devices in lieu of or in addition to break tanks can also be installed to prevent contamination back to the domestic water supply. These are certified and calibrated every 12 months to ensure their effectiveness. The engineering consultant will advise on this matter.

Laboratory liquid wastes are connected to a dilution pit through chemical resistant pipes such as glass, polypropylene or a material to resist the waste being discharged. The disposal of solvents down the sink and through waste pipes is prohibited in many jurisdictions so the engineering consultant will advise on this matter.

Laboratory sinks can be installed in island benches even when the waste cannot be discharged down through the floor. Both pump-out and vacuum extraction systems have been installed successfully allowing wastes to extend vertically from the sink to the ceiling above and thence horizontally to the service duct.

The design of the laboratory waste management is one of the most important issues and needs to be determined at an early stage. It will have many implications on space requirements.

The hardest decision in laboratory services design is the extent of the initial provision. Do you provide services only to the outlets requested or to the whole building? We generally design the building structure to accommodate a services infrastructure and install the main lines and as many branch lines as necessary for initial requirements.

Chapter 5

Special cabinets and benches

5.1 Fume cupboards

Operations involving the use or generation of flammable liquids, gases, airborne irritants, poisons or sensitising agents, etc. should be carried out in a fume cupboard to contain the hazard. Their manufactured design and installation is controlled by standards and regulations. While manufacturers are aware of these requirements it is essential for those responsible for arranging the position of fume cupboards also to be aware of all the regulations, including the location of fume cupboards in relation to workbenches, doors, columns, etc.

As the materials handled within fume cupboards represent one of the highest fire risk elements in the laboratory, fume cupboards should not be located on the fire escape routes, should be furthest from exits and therefore ideally located at the perimeter window wall. In this location the exhaust ducts can be external which has advantages in terms of fire control (see cover). The location of exhaust ducts to the roof, stack location and height are a site environment issue and the local building and health authorities will have to approve the design.

I recommend that the design team should contact all manufacturers and have their representatives describe the various features of their designs to ascertain which design suits the laboratory use.

Some of the features which are favoured by laboratory staff are:

a. A level worksurface as opposed to one which is graded to a sink.
b. Allowing adequate knee space for working close to the cupboard, which is only available if the water and gas controls are on the side frame.
c. Good lighting within the cupboard as recommended by the fume cupboard standard in the country.

d. A steel frame supporting the cupboard to allow access to the underside of the cupboard for maintenance and alterations and access for wheelchair operators as illustrated in Figure 4.8.

e. A walk-in fume cupboard for tall apparatus such as distillation.

Energy conservation can be achieved in fume cupboard design by a device to control the velocity of the air flow across the sash at all sash positions to the minimum safe capture velocity stipulated by the fume cupboard standards.

5.2 Local exhaust ventilation

It is better in terms of occupational health, safety and energy conservation to extract hazardous airborne contaminants, e.g. fumes, dust, mists, vapours, etc., at the source before it dissipates into the laboratory environment. Once it has spread it will have to be removed from the general laboratory exhaust air.

There are proprietary products with adjustable hoods and flexible ducting which can be installed within reach of the workbench where the extraction is needed. These products can exhaust contaminants to the outside air or be portable with filters to recycle the extracted air.

Lateral exhaust ducts can be built behind dedicated benches to provide excellent operator access and contaminant control.

Local exhaust ventilators are not an alternative to fume cupboards.

5.3 Biological safety cabinets

Biological safety cabinets are designed to contain material, often living micro-organisms, and thereby protect the laboratory user from exposure to aerosols produced from handling the material.

The cabinets contain fans which pass the recycled air through HEPA filters.

There are several products available and the company representatives can advise on their product performance and cost.

Draught-free locations are essential.

5.4 Laminar flow cabinets

Laminar flow cabinets provide a clean space within which a product can be handled without fear of contamination to that product by introduced agents. Typical applications include pharmaceutical products and packaging, media preparation, food technology, electronics assembly and plant research.

Laminar flow cabinets are manufactured by the same suppliers as biological safety cabinets. Draught-free locations are essential.

5.5 Down-draught benches

The small scale dissection of human and animal tissue which has been fixed or preserved, e.g. in Formalin, is an unsafe task if the formaldehyde vapour is inhaled by the operator. By exhausting this vapour downwards below the specimen being dissected, exposure to the tissue fixative is controlled. Figure 5.1 shows a design for a down-draught bench which I have used in anatomical pathology. Other designs are also based on the same principle that local exhaust ventilation should not exhaust airborne contaminants towards or past the operator's nose.

5.6 Flammable liquids cabinets

Special proprietary product cabinets are made for storage of flammable liquids within the laboratory. They conform in their capacity and construction to standards and regulations and should have their certification displayed on the cabinets.

Because of the potential fire hazard these cabinets should be used only when essential for the storage of chemicals within the laboratory when a bulk store has not been provided adjacent to the laboratory and when storage facilities outside the laboratory would lead to unnecessary risks in carrying chemicals back and forth or the store material is required on a daily/weekly short-term basis. One solution is a trolley cabinet, wheeled out into a fire resistant store overnight. Minimum cabinet spacing and proximity to ignition sources are defined by standards and regulations.

5.7 Decanting benches

There is a risk of accidental exposure when decanting from a large container to smaller bottles for laboratory use. If the decanting is done on a bench similar to the bench as described under 5.5 but with local exhaust ventilation, the vapour will not affect the operator. If there is a spill the liquid will fall directly into the sink bowl which should have at least the capacity of the largest container supplied.

5.8 Anti-vibration benches

Some equipment and instruments need to be placed on a bench which is isolated from structure-borne vibrations, e.g. micro balances. Typical vibrations are those created by heavy road or rail traffic, air-conditioning plant and, in material testing laboratories, mechanical hammers and tensile testing machines.

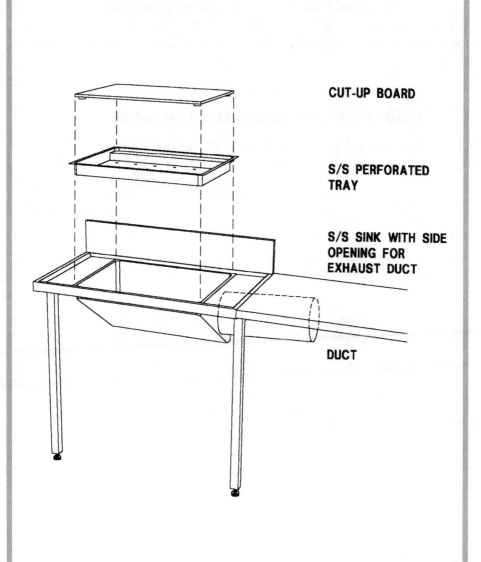

CUT-UP BOARD

S/S PERFORATED TRAY

S/S SINK WITH SIDE OPENING FOR EXHAUST DUCT

DUCT

Figure 5.1 Down-draught bench showing the exhaust ventilation duct from the sink below the dissection board

Microscopes and balances are both sensitive to vibrations, although the trend in design is for these instruments to have built-in vibration isolating bases.

Figure 4.7 shows a design for an anti-vibration bench which is in three main components, a heavy bench top, pure rubber elastomeric pads and a steel frame. The very heavy components can be carried separately, making the bench as movable as any other workbench. The bench top thickness allows for knee space if the operator is seated.

5.9 Equipment/instrumentation benches

Some equipment needs to be supported at a different height to normal 900 mm high workbenches. For example, some large bench-mounted auto-analysers have controls and vision panels at the top and need to be supported at a level to suit the various heights of laboratory staff. Biohazard cabinets are best mounted on lower benches which allow the bench height within the cabinet to be level with adjacent benches. Both these examples call for an adjustable-height bench.

Figure 4.4 shows a typical adjustable bench which can be mechanically wound up and down between 900 mm and 750 mm height.

Adjustable workbenches are useful to provide staff with the option of working at desk height or bench height and for disabled staff. These desk/benches are used in conjunction with adjustable height chairs/stools.

Chapter 6

Laboratory instrumentation and equipment

6.1 Instrumentation for analysis and testing

The design brief will describe the laboratory instrumentation proposed for the new laboratory. Some will undoubtedly be existing in their present premises, so these can be examined for support and services. The rest will be new so details of the support benches and services required can be obtained from brochures and the supplier's representative.

Under 4.1 – Workbenches, I mentioned the benches designed to support HPLC instruments.

The design of laboratory analysers and test equipment is changing constantly and their accommodation needs to be adaptable to facilitate the changes. The trend is also unpredictable from the present trend of combining several functions into one very large floor-standing machine, to robotic design or to miniature components. Manufacturers are trying to keep up with the constant demand from scientists for equipment to perform new tasks. Some of the new equipment is several metres in length, calling for very flexible laboratory space.

Under 4.1 and 4.5 – Laboratory services, I describe a 'bollard' system I designed for maximum flexibility. Plates 1, 4 and 14 and Figure 4.2 show a laboratory with floor-standing instrumentation and movable benches assembled around a bollard to which the instruments are connected for their power and gas needs. Plate 3 shows another laboratory where a services 'pendant' is suspended from the ceiling and the instruments are connected to it in much the same way. This design obstructs a clear view across the laboratory and I have found that laboratory staff do not favour a 'cluttered' appearance.

6.2 Centrifuges

Centrifuges revolve at variable speeds to separate components by centrifugal force and can be quite noisy. The larger models which are generally floor-standing are sometimes accommodated in separate rooms to insulate the sound and vibration. They are used for separations and clarifications.

6.3 Ovens and autoclaves

Ovens and autoclaves are used in a variety of laboratories and the different models are manufactured to suit the particular requirements of the laboratory work. Improved models do not radiate the heat of earlier designs as more efficient insulating material has become available to the manufacturers. However, the client may want to install old equipment in the new laboratory. It is good practice to locate ovens against a wall, away from the general workbenches or even in a separate room as they can still generate very high heat loads. If the oven has a flue it is easier to install the flue against a wall.

High temperature ovens, muffle furnaces and autoclaves ideally need to be located under canopy hoods to remove heat load and odours, and also shielded to prevent radiant heat.

6.4 Incubators

Normally in microbiology laboratories with a clean air environment and sometimes used for seed germination, growth and culture experimentation, incubators are designed for specific laboratory work. They are generally floor-standing but under-bench models are also available. Free air circulation to the cooling/heating equipment is required especially if located close to or under workbenches. Walk-in incubator rooms are also common.

6.5 Refrigerators and cool rooms

Refrigerators for laboratories are designed to fit under workbenches or may be large floor-standing cabinets with solid or glass doors. The design brief will nominate the type.

Cool rooms and freezers for laboratories are generally standard models of prefabricated insulated panel construction. However, the design brief may call for more sophisticated equipment with better temperature and humidity controls which will be specially assembled for the laboratory. The shelving required will need to withstand the harsh conditions of the atmosphere in the coolroom.

If frequent access to cool rooms is required, the alternative design solution of a series of glass-fronted cabinets instead of one large space should be considered. However, these stand-alone cabinets do generate a heat load from their individual cooling systems, which would have to be mentioned in the brief and allowed for in the air-conditioning design. The design brief should also nominate uninterrupted power supply to these cabinets to protect the samples contained.

The design I sometimes recommend is the 'supermarket' cool room with a series of glass front doors for convenient access to shelves within the cool room, and with one large door for more infrequent and wider access for trolleys and trays.

Chapter 7

On completion

7.1 Commissioning equipment

7.2 Security

7.3 Emergency procedures

7.4 Services controls and emergencies

7.5 Building manual

7.6 As-built drawings

7.7 Joint final inspections

7.1 Commissioning equipment

A commissioning meeting(s) should be held at the equipment location and attended by the supplier/installer to explain the operation of the equipment to the laboratory staff and client's maintenance engineers.

Most of the equipment will be installed by the supplier. They will have provided all the necessary information on the services to be connected to the equipment by the electrical, mechanical and hydraulic subcontractors.

The supplier may insist on making the final connections to the equipment or the connections may be left to the subcontractors, who should also attend the commissioning meeting.

The laboratory staff should be shown how the equipment operates and what are their responsibilities for its proper use and maintenance. It is the supplier's responsibility under Quality Assurance to describe common failure of the equipment and the remedial action to be taken by staff. Suppliers have statutory obligations to disclose and supply safe operating procedures. The equipment manual should be studied by the staff and any questions put to the supplier at the commissioning meeting.

7.2 Security

The degree and extent of security will be described in the design brief as mentioned in 1.14 – Security. Staff should be thoroughly familiar with the security system which should be shown and explained to them by both the security system installation contractor and the company's own security staff. The alarm drill should be acted out so that all staff have experienced a break in security and performed the appropriate counter-action.

7.3 Emergency procedures

The evacuation plan in the event of fire, chemical spills, bomb threat, medical emergency, etc. should be developed as part of the design process, fully documented and displayed in all laboratories showing the alternative escape routes from that particular laboratory to the assembly points outside the building. The displays are best designed with the consultation of the relevant authorities and produced by the client building owner on a copy of the building plan.

As soon as the building is initially occupied, staff should be fully informed of their responsibility in the event of an emergency, observing the source of a fire or when the alarm has been sounded by others.

The fire extinguishers installed in the laboratories and elsewhere, as recommended by the fire prevention authority, should be demonstrated to all staff by the supplier.

When all staff are thoroughly conversant with fire procedures the management should arrange in cooperation with the fire brigade a fire drill exercise when they know that all staff will be present.

7.4 Services controls and emergencies

Provision will have been made in the reticulation of laboratory power, gases and water for isolation of sections of the installation in the event of an emergency or routine maintenance.

These control valves and circuit breakers should be clearly identified and shown to all staff on occupation of the site. The reasons for their provision should be explained to them by discussing possible scenarios when the staff will have to activate the shut-down control.

7.5 Building manual

The building contractor should supply to the building owner a manual containing all the technical information provided to them by equipment and material suppliers and subcontractors. If the manual is not complete to the building owner's satisfaction he should insist on the contractor obtaining the missing data. Apart from the obvious items, such as laboratory equipment which has been mentioned under 7.1 – Commissioning equipment, it is necessary to know the supplier of all the building components, such as filters, fluorescent tubes, etc., so that matching replacements can be reordered from the same supplier.

7.6 As-built drawings

The building contractor should supply to the building owner 'as-built' drawings. These drawings will be the original drawings for the building contract but will have been revised to reflect the many variations which are inevitably made during the course of construction.

Contractors try to avoid this onerous responsibility if the tender documents called for as-built drawings to be provided, and need a reminder or two. The building structure may not have been altered much but the mechanical services, air-conditioning duct work, hydraulic lines, etc. will have been altered considerably from the tender documents where they are frequently only diagrammatic.

From my experience, building owners rarely have building plans, and if so, they are seldom up to date, as the laboratory is altered continuously, often in an ad-hoc manner.

7.7 Joint final inspections

When the builder has completed all of the above, all building and equipment defects and malfunctions have been rectified, local authorities have given permission for occupation and the builder is ready to hand over all the premises, a formal joint meeting or meetings must be held. Official representation from the architects, engineering consultants, main contractor, all services subcontractors, all suppliers/installers of equipment, should walk around the building with the client, services manager and maintenance staff and explain everything they need to know for the proper function of the building.

These meetings would include items mentioned under 7.1–7.6 and 8.1–8.5.

At this time a list of contact names and telephone numbers for emergencies should be given to the client.

Chapter 8

Maintenance

8.1 Bench tops

There are no bench top materials which do not require periodic cleaning. The degree and frequency of cleaning will depend on the type of bench top material. The resistance to the sort of use, be it abrasive as in material testing laboratories or chemical spills, will have been taken into account in the selection at the design stage.

It now becomes a management and staff decision on how clean to maintain the bench tops. Most laboratory managers insist on chemical spills being wiped off immediately before they stain. Turning the cold water on before emptying chemicals into the sink will also reduce staining. A client of mine decided, with the staff, that each member would clean their own benchspace every Friday night, thereby maintaining a very high degree of cleanliness. The process takes, on average, only a few minutes.

The manual referred to in 7.5 – Building manual, should include instructions by the bench top manufacturer for cleaning their particular product.

8.2 Flooring

Access to laboratories by cleaning staff needs careful consideration. Laboratories using radioisotopes, for example, should not be cleaned routinely but by special staff. Other laboratories to be cleaned by staff or contractors need also to be given clear instructions on what spaces they can clean and what wastes they can empty.

The flooring in laboratories is mentioned under 3.4 – Interior design, and if a pre-finished vinyl sheeting has been installed the cleaning will be quite easy. As the laboratory is air conditioned there will be only the dust and fibres brought in on clothing. A fine spray of detergent and a wipe clean with a floor mop should be all that is required each night. The manual referred to under 7.5 – Building manual, should include instructions by the flooring product manufacturer for cleaning the particular flooring installed. If cleaning contractors are involved it is most important to instruct them accordingly, otherwise they will use the heavy rotary scrubbers which can remove the polyurethane finish on the flooring. They may also apply a polish which is unnecessary and will collect dirt.

The floor is easier to clean if under-bench cupboards and drawer units are movable and not suspended above the floor. The storage units can be pulled out into the aisle leaving plenty of space to clean right through under the bench.

Cleaning staff should also be informed of the hazards they are likely to encounter in the laboratories.

8.3 Filters

There are filters in air-handling equipment such as biohazard cabinets, recycling fume cabinets and clean room filters which need to be monitored and replaced when exhausted. These are another item which should be included in the building manual.

8.4 Waste disposal

The systems for disposal of waste will typically include laboratory liquid waste from sinks to the dilution pit prior to release into the authority's sewers, having prior approval from that authority.

Other systems of waste disposal include containers within the laboratory for infectious waste, sharps, protective clothing for laundering, etc. which are carried out by specialist waste management contractors.

Solvent waste is one of the most hazardous, requiring experienced professional design and may be one of the following two alternatives. The waste can be discharged into a dedicated sink and gravitate to a collection tank with both tank and waste mechanically ventilated to prevent an explosive atmosphere. Alternatively solvent waste can be returned to winchesters and placed in a solvent store for collection by a contractor. Either way, appropriate maintenance for collection will be essential.

The proper maintenance of laboratory waste systems is probably the most important maintenance responsibility of the laboratory staff.

8.5 Safety stations

The health and safety equipment at the safety stations in laboratories needs routine maintenance and replacement if necessary. For instance, safety showers should be regularly activated with a bucket under the shower head and use-by dates checked on fire extinguishers.

8.6 Laboratory services and equipment

There are a number of other laboratory services and equipment that require maintenance. Some examples are fume cupboards, luminaires, vacuum and air-compressors, demineralised water and local exhaust ventilation systems. The design team needs to be aware of the complexity of laboratory maintenance issues and to seek the client's instructions at the briefing stage.

I recommend that a 2 year service agreement is included in the contract with equipment suppliers.

Case studies

The case studies illustrate several architects' solutions to the need for flexibility and other laboratory client requirements.

Case studies 1, 6, 7, 9, 11, 14, 16 and 17 were selected for provision of accessible spaces for maintenance and future change to laboratory services. Case studies 6 and 17 are examples of interstitial spaces between laboratory floors.

Case study 1 is an example of flexibility in university research laboratories showing the 'generic' layout which can be readily adapted to suit all disciplines as the need for expansion and contraction of departments will occur in the future.

Case studies 1, 6, 12, 13, 15, 16 and 17 were selected for their atria and other shared spaces where professional interaction can occur

Case study 4 is particularly interesting for the planning of circulation and support facilities to ensure that staff will meet during the course of their work.

Case study 8 is included for the unusual brief in terms of the desired spatial relationships of laboratories and support facilities.

Case study 9 is included as an example of laboratories traditionally separate, now sharing an open-planned space successfully.

Case study 12 is an example of overhead servicing to laboratory benches and equipment in a heritage building where the usual services infrastructure is not available and the client required maximum flexibility.

Readers should contact the nominated architects in each case study for further information on the design and construction participants.

1 Biology teaching and research building, University of Wollongong, NSW.

2 Biological Sciences & Biomedical Engineering, University of New South Wales, Sydney, NSW.

3 Children's Medical Research Foundation, Westmead, NSW.

4 Centenary Institute of Cancer Medicine & Cell Biology, Sydney, NSW.

5 SmithKline Beecham International Laboratories, Consumer Healthcare, Ermington, NSW.

6 Life Sciences Building, Ciba Pharmaceuticals Division, Summit, New Jersey, USA.

7 Pacific Power Research Laboratories, University of Newcastle, NSW.

8 BHP Research Laboratories, Newcastle, NSW.

9 Central West Pathology Services, Orange, NSW.

10 CSIRO McMasters Laboratories, Prospect, NSW.

11 ANSTO Radiopharmaceutical Laboratory, Lucas Heights, NSW.

12 Centre for Proteome Research and Gene-Product Mapping, National Innovation Centre, Australian Technology Park, Everleigh, NSW.

13 Garvan Institute of Medical Research, Sydney, NSW.

14 ACTEW Corporation Laboratories, Fyshwick, ACT.

15 Camelia Botnar Laboratories, Great Ormond Street Hospital, London, England.

16 Institute of Medical Science, The University of Aberdeen, Scotland.

17 Therapeutic Goods Administration (TGA), Symonston, ACT.

I would like to thank the following photographers for contributing the photographs used in the colour plate sections:

    Brett Boardman for plates 20 and 21
    Camera Vision for plates 1, 4, 11, 12, 13, 14, 16 and 17
    Mike Chorley for plates 3, 18 and 19
    Peter Hyatt for plates 7, 8 and 9
    Alf Manciager for plate 15
    Eric Sierins of Max Dupain & Associates for plates 10, 22 and 23
    University of Aberdeen Imaging Dept. for plate 27

Case study 1

Biology teaching and research building
University of Wollongong, NSW

Architect and Laboratory Design Consultant   Brian C. Griffin

The brief for this building included two important requirements. The teaching laboratories had to be multi-discipline for undergraduate students in biology, nursing and other future courses. The post-graduate research facilities were to be arranged in five separate groups including offices for the supervisors in multi-discipline generic laboratories.

The 3-D drawings IE and IF show the design solution for the flexible teaching laboratories. Student benches are adjustable from bench height to allow sitting on stools and standing to desk height for microscopy seated on chairs. Twenty-four laboratory gases, power, data, water and waste services are provided at the benches from floor-standing services bollards.

The floor plans show the teaching laboratories and lecture theatre which generate the most traffic located adjacent to the level 1 entry and the stair to level 2.

Level 2 (Case study 1B) has a dual corridor plan with research laboratories on the perimeter and laboratory support facilities in the core, accessible from both corridors.

The cross-sections show the sub-floor area for services reticulation and the air-conditioning plant room over the level 2 support facilities, which have a lower ceiling height requirement than the research laboratories.

The photograph of the building (Plate 6) shows the external adjustable louvres which restrict sunlight to a safe level. The louvres are designed to be adjusted automatically by light sensors.

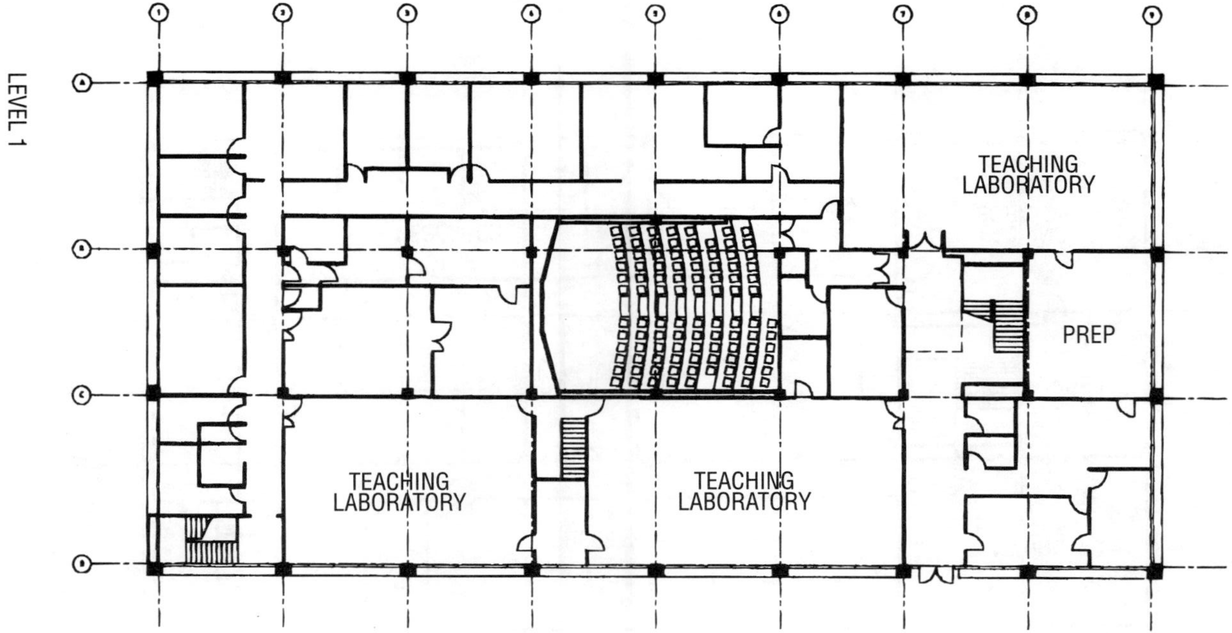

LEVEL 1

TEACHING LABORATORY

PREP

TEACHING LABORATORY

TEACHING LABORATORY

Case study IA Level I floor plan (continued overleaf)

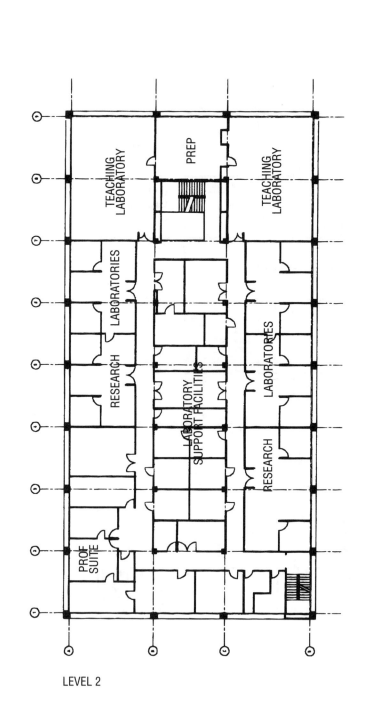

LEVEL 2

Case study 1B Level 2 floor plan

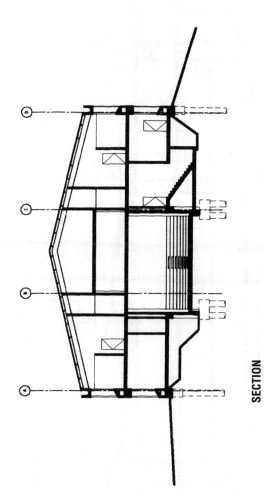

SECTION

Case study 1C Section *(continued overleaf)*

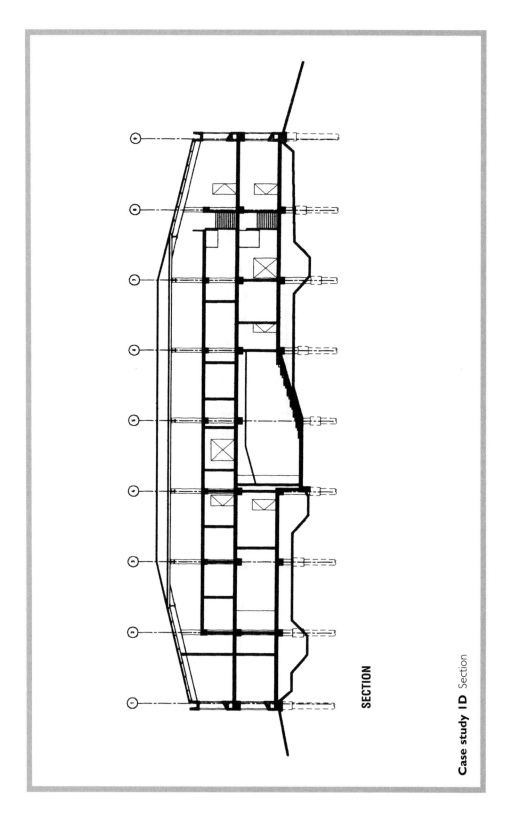

SECTION

Case study 1D Section

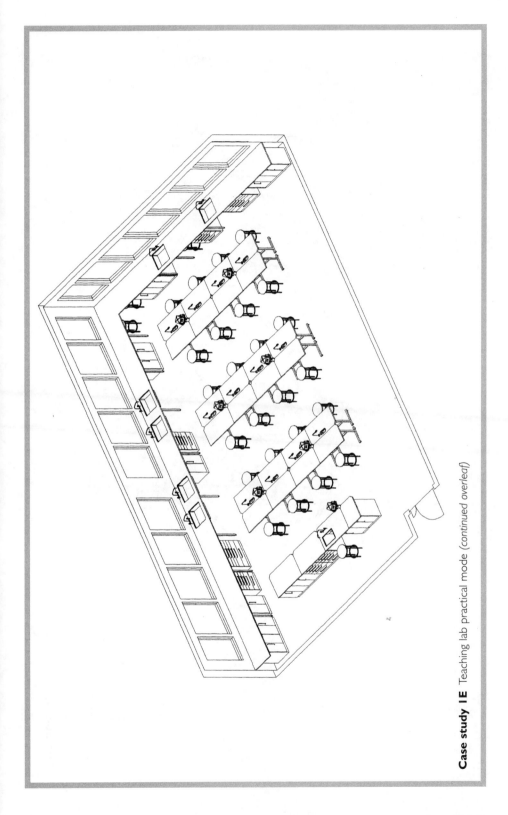

Case study 1E Teaching lab practical mode *(continued overleaf)*

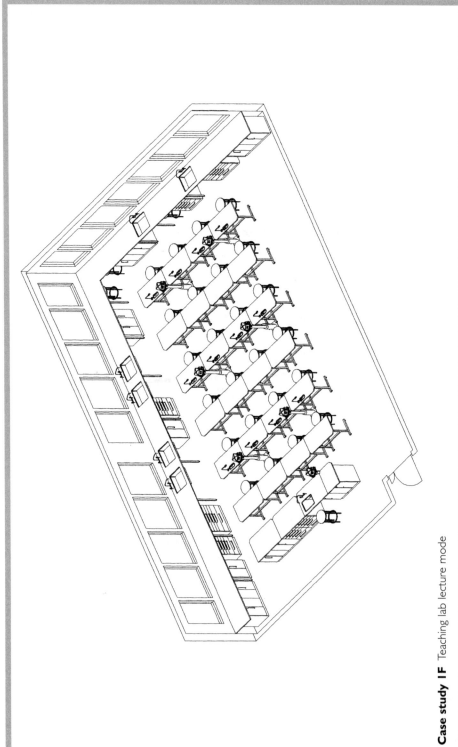

Case study 1F Teaching lab lecture mode

Case study 2

Biological Sciences & Biomedical Engineering University of NSW

Architects   Laurence Nield & Partners
            Director in charge   Tony Fisher
            Project architects   Neil Greenstreet
                              Neil Hanson
                              Robert Yuen

The site determined the urban form of the building, the curving road producing a curving pointed plan at the east end of the building. The architectural treatment, the scales and rhythms of the building resulted from this sensitive and careful contextual analysis. The framed concrete structures of the north campus, particularly the Mathews Building, were echoed in the framed articulation in the cast aluminium screens on the new building.

The rhythms of the in situ concrete of the neighbouring buildings were repeated in the vertical aluminium wall panels of the new building. Furthermore, the colour and textures of the neighbouring brick lecture theatres to the east were continued in the lowest floor of the Samuels Building using brick, which both continued the 'materiality' of the ground and was a more robust material than the metal cladding, enabling a logical division of walling materials as well as making an important contextual link. The cast aluminium sun screens were used as a layering, scale-making device to emphasise the density of the street alignments of the building and the formal order of the building frame. At the top, the building 'dematerialises' into the glass house which will soon be filled with plants, providing an extraordinary capping to the building. This might even be used as a 'winter garden' for the building users: a facility to draw occupants to the top.

At either end, the building 'slides' into terraces, exterior staff amenity areas, 'promenade decks' for laboratory staff to seek relief from their exacting tasks.

The planning is simple and logical and is immediately recognisable to any visitor or occupant of the building. Laboratories on one side of the corridor, offices, cool rooms, cores, etc. on the other. Four central stacks down the length of this corridor carry the laboratory plumbing, sanitary plumbing, storm water drainage, electrical risers and cupboards, and exhaust ductwork for fume cupboards and special laboratory exhausts.

Typical laboratory floors, such as level 1 and level 4, have large glazed panels between the laboratories and corridors. This lets good daylight into the corridors, alleviating the tunnel feeling so common with a double-loaded corridor. It also serves to expose the workers in the laboratories to the corridor. This is useful in a teaching instruction university. It is also an important safety feature; people in trouble dealing with hazardous chemicals, etc. can readily be seen by passers-by and students' activities can be readily monitored. The glass in these windows is wired glass in accordance with fire safety guidelines for escape corridors in educational institutions, while lending some intricacy and texture to the view.

In a building that can have environmental conditions ranging from a full level naturally ventilated to individual laboratories with absolute filtration for incoming conditioned air and for exhaust air (100% exhaust), the energy considerations are limited to a structure/envelope having good thermal mass and insulation, centralised energy systems to achieve economies of scale and providing for heat recovery in areas where conditioned air is fully exhausted without recirculation. Laboratory and Animal House exhausts are discharged at high level in accordance with current regulations, taking account of established wind patterns and adjacent built forms.

(See also Plates 7, 8 and 9 in the colour section.)

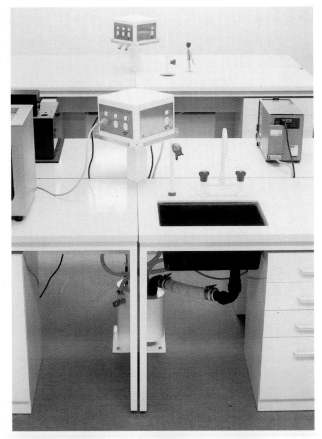

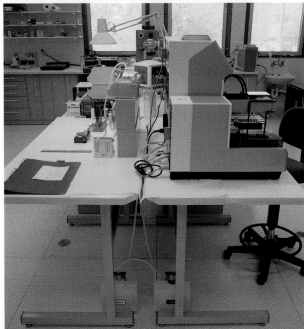

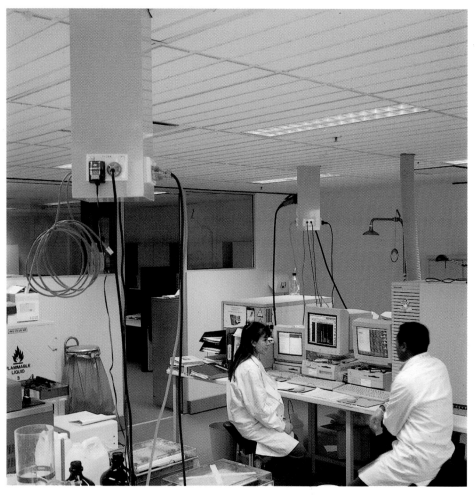

Plate 3 Typical laboratory with pendant bollards servicing instrumentation showing the high degree of flexibility with no fixed elements on the floor

Plate 4 Typical laboratory with floor-standing bollards, showing the flexibility of movable benches and floor-standing or bench-mounted equipment ▶

Plate 5 Typical laboratory with instrumentation on movable benches showing the variety of movable units ▼

◀ **Plate 6** (Case study 1) Biology teaching and research building. University of Wollongong, NSW, external automatic sun control

◀ **Plate 7** (Case study 2) Biological Sciences & Biomedical Engineering, University of New South Wales, Sydney, NSW, external view

▲ **Plate 8** (Case study 2) Biological Sciences & Biomedical Engineering, University of New South Wales, Sydney, NSW, external view

Plate 9 (Case study 2) Biological Sciences & Biomedical Engineering, University of New South Wales, Sydney, NSW, external view ▶

Plate 10 (Case study 3) Children's Medical Research Foundation, Westmead, NSW, atrium ▶

Plate 11 (Case study 4) Centenary Institute of Cancer Medicine & Cell Biology, Sydney, NSW, typical movable workbenches and write-up

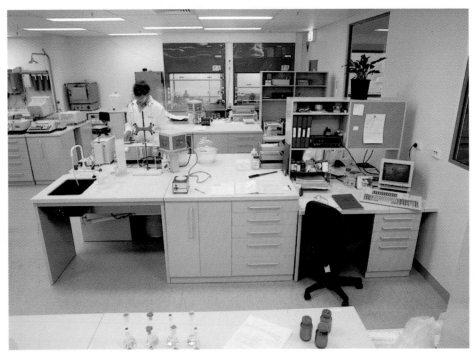

Plate 12 (Case study 5) SmithKline Beecham International Laboratories, Consumer Healthcare, Ermington, NSW, typical movable workbenches and write-up

◀ **Plate 13** (Case study 5) SmithKline Beecham International Laboratories, Consumer Healthcare, Ermington, NSW, services bollards and movable benches

◀ **Plate 14** (Case study 7) Pacific Power Research Laboratories, University of Newcastle, NSW, typical laboratory with services bollards, movable benches and floor-standing equipment

Plate 15 (Case study 9) Central West Pathology Services, Orange, NSW, floor-standing equipment and movable workbenches ▼

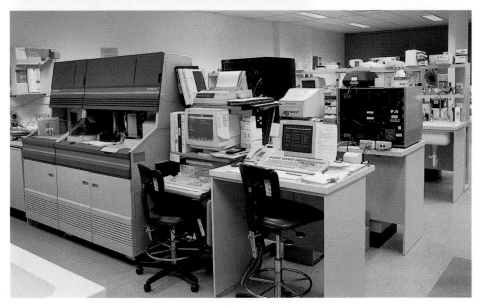

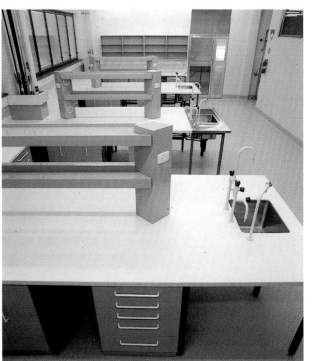

◀ **Plate 16** (Case study 10)
CSIRO McMasters Laboratories,
Fyshwick, ACT, typical
laboratory with free space for
floor-standing equipment
against the inside wall .

Plate 17 (Case study 10)
CSIRO McMasters Laboratories,
Fyshwick, ACT, typical
laboratory workbench with
movable under-bench storage
units ▼

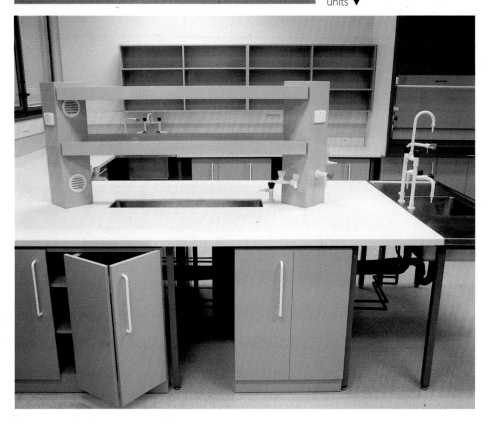

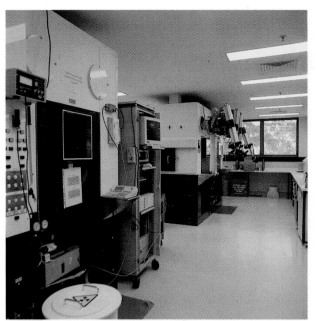

◀ **Plate 18** (Case study 11) ANSTO Radiopharmaceutical Laboratory, Lucas Heights, NSW, automation laboratory

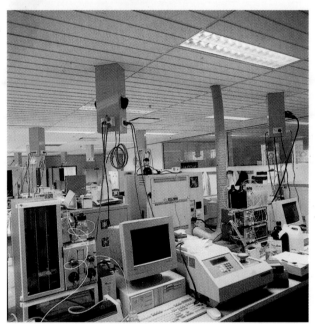

◀ **Plate 19** (Case study 12) Centre for Proteome Research and Gene-Product Mapping, National Innovation Centre, Australian Technology Park, Everleigh, NSW, laboratory benches and equipment serviced from ceiling pendant bollards

▲ **Plate 20** (Case study 12) Centre for Proteome Research and Gene-Product Mapping, National Innovation Centre, Australian Technology Park, Everleigh, NSW, heritage listed building

Plate 21 (Case study 12) Centre for Proteome Research and Gene-Product Mapping, National Innovation Centre, Australian Technology Park, Everleigh, NSW, atrium ▶

Plate 22 (Case study 13) Garvan Institute of Medical Research, Sydney, NSW, atrium roof and laboratories ▶

Plate 23 (Case study 13) Garvan Institute of Medical Research, Sydney, NSW, atrium and library ▶

Plate 24 (Case study 14) ACTEW Corporation Laboratories, Fyshwick, ACT, typical laboratory interior showing fume cupboards integrated with movable benches ▼

▲ **Plate 25** (Case study 14) ACTEW Corporation Laboratories, Fyshwick, ACT, exterior view from main entry

▲ **Plate 26** (Case study 15) Great Ormond Street Hospital, coffee bars at each level in atrium

▲ **Plate 27** (Case study 16) Institute of Medical Science, The University of Aberdeen

▲ **Plate 28** (Case study 17) Therapeutic Goods Administration (TGA), Symonston, ACT, aerial view of laboratory complex

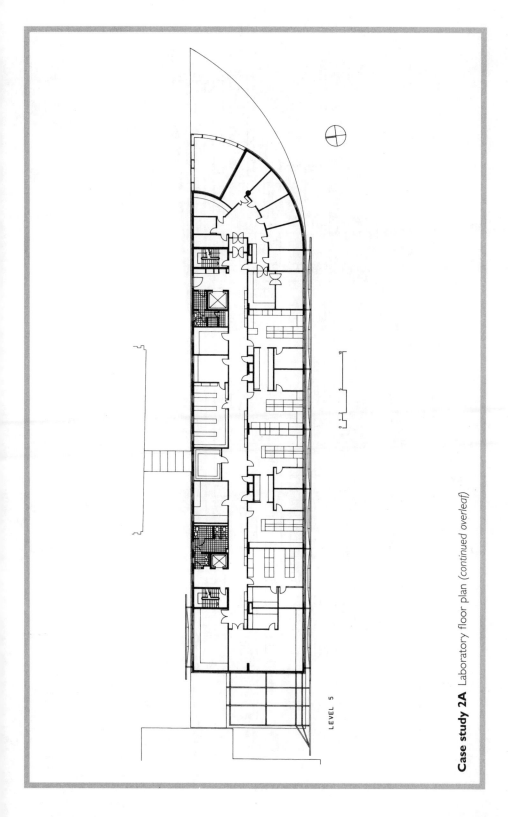

LEVEL 5

Case study 2A Laboratory floor plan *(continued overleaf)*

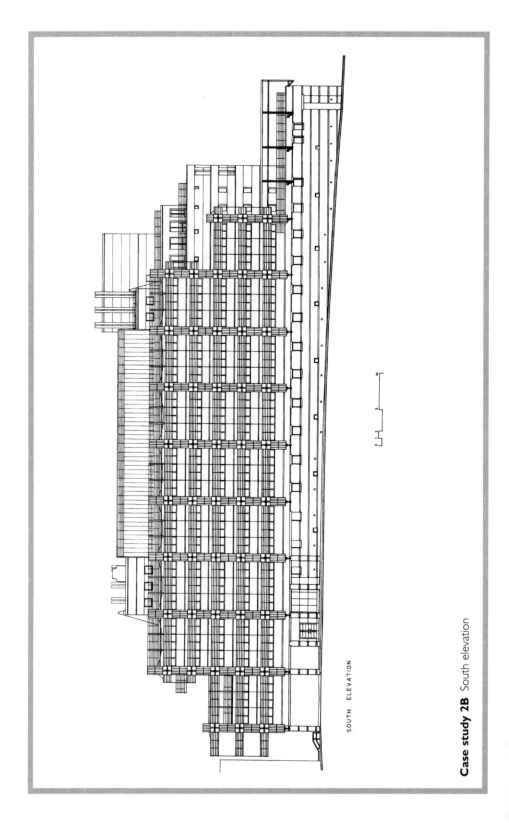

SOUTH ELEVATION

Case study 2B South elevation

Case study 3

Children's Medical Research Foundation
Westmead, NSW

Architects   Ancher Mortlock Woolley Pty Ltd
        Project Directors   Ken Woolley
                      Dale Swan

The building is 4500 m² in total area over two floors and has 12 major laboratory spaces. The design was to include a strategy for adding at least four laboratories to be built without disruption to the work at a cost of $11.5 million and was completed in 1992.

The brief required the research facility to be capable of a stand-alone operation but should facilitate research interaction with various members of staff of the adjacent Children's Hospital. The site/building should be highly visible to the public with special consideration given to the Library and its links with the Central Libraries at Westmead.

The plan form has a central core of support areas surrounded by groups of four laboratories. There is a perimeter corridor between the two areas providing working access to the support facilities and freezer holding areas as well as compartmenting the plan in accordance with the regulations.

The cross corridors provide centralised access to the ground floor areas with the most critical support areas in the centre. The symmetrical plan arrangement enables a maximum distance of 50 metres for interaction and movement to be achieved. The plan form also facilitates the addition of four laboratories on the northern face without disruption to the building.

The ground floor is smaller in area and hence withdrawn from the perimeter of the building. This provides sunshading for the ground floor and articulates the façade, defines the different areas of activity in the building and reinforces the low scale.

The plan is organised to secure the laboratory activities in the building where food, make-up, etc. cannot be taken. The lobby is the interface between the public and laboratory activities with direct access to the directorate, administration and conference facilities. The delivery dock has direct access to the stores areas and can be directly supervised by the administration department. It also allows controlled external access to the stores areas and can be directly supervised by the administration department. It also allows controlled external access for maintenance.

The illustration shows the quadrant shaped atrium with a central access stair which provides a focal and orientation element within the symmetrical plan. The service lift opens into this area.

The library and lunch room have a sun facing orientation, the library is both accessible from the secure and public areas of the building.

The overall form is an expression of the different activities in the building; the central support facilities with central plant room and atrium light, and the laboratory groups. This composition is further defined by elements such as the escape stairs, conference rooms and the sunshading and roof support systems, together with finer detailing of trims, margins, etc.

(See also Plate 10 in the colour section.)

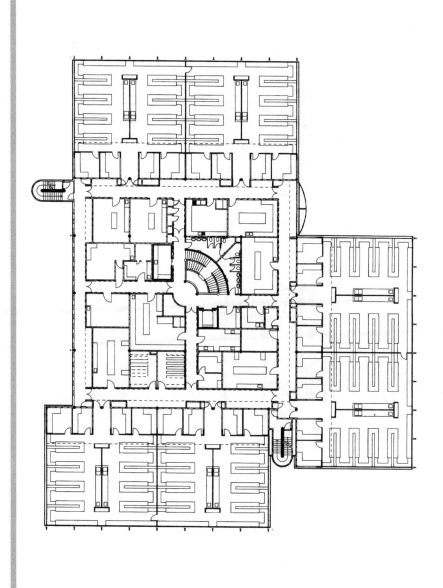

Case study 3A Laboratory floor plan *(continued overleaf)*

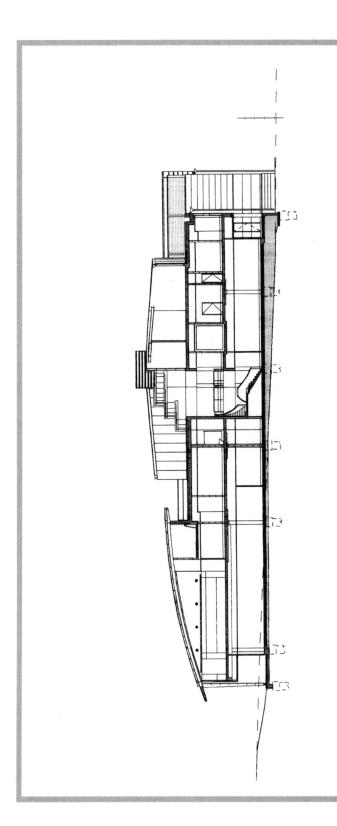

Case study 3B Section

Case study 4

Centenary Institute of Cancer Medicine & Cell Biology
Sydney, NSW

Architects   Brown Brewer & Gregory
            Project Architect   Mark Boffa

The design philosophy was to create functional and flexible spaces in a manner that would allow additions and alterations resulting from changing needs and evolving research technology, to be carried out economically and with minimum disruption to ongoing activity. The laboratory spaces were to be spacious enough to accommodate a complete research unit, yet small enough to provide peace, privacy and human scale.

The rectangular plan consists of a centrally located core, with a laboratory module in each of the outer 'corners'. Opposing laboratories are separated by the core of ancillary function rooms. Flexibility is provided with movable benches in configurations which do not interrupt circulation or workflow. By eliminating the traditional central corridor and combining the general circulation space with the laboratories the plan is more compact without compromising the function of the areas or walking distances to support facilities.

The core ancillary areas are configured to be shared between two laboratory modules. Cross corridors are reduced to a minimum and rooms arranged so that they open alternately into opposing laboratories. The effect of this is that while shared rooms can only be accessed from one of the two modules they serve, and members of one team have to walk through to the other side to access some of the core areas, discussion and research interaction is encouraged, especially when rooms are shared by both teams at once.

The benches are at a right angle to the window wall. The bench at the window is an adjustable height worktop, used by some researchers at desk height and others at bench height as an extension of the laboratory bench. The laboratory furniture is modular and movable, with all services in a services spine between the benches.

Reticulation of services along the external walls, within vertical and horizontal ducts is accessible through removable panels for alterations and maintenance. The laboratory spaces do not have ceilings, and all high level services are exposed and colour coded for ease of identification; the result is a volume which is more comfortable to work in and which provides a variety otherwise limited by traditional laboratory designs.

(See also Plate 11 in the colour section.)

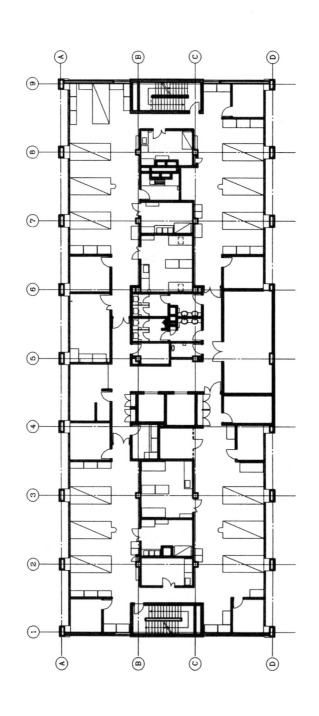

Case study 4A Laboratory floor plan

Case study 5

SmithKline Beecham International Laboratories
Consumer Healthcare
Ermington, NSW

Architect and Laboratory Design Consultant   Brian C. Griffin

The brief called for maximum flexibility in the accommodation for the quality assurance programme. The space for the instrumentation including auto-analysis, HPLC and atomic absorption had to allow the rearrangement of equipment on benches and the possible future floor-standing equipment.

The solution was to arrange modular movable benches around floor standing services bollards installed on a regular grid. The modular units included workstations at desk height which were originally placed at the window wall but could be placed anywhere the staff required.

Small rinse sinks are provided on some benches, including some for instrumentation waste, but a central washing facility with autoclaves was planned at the far corner. The fume cupboards were also located at the far corner, furthest from the exits, and not on the fire egress route.

(See also Plates 12 and 13 in the colour section.)

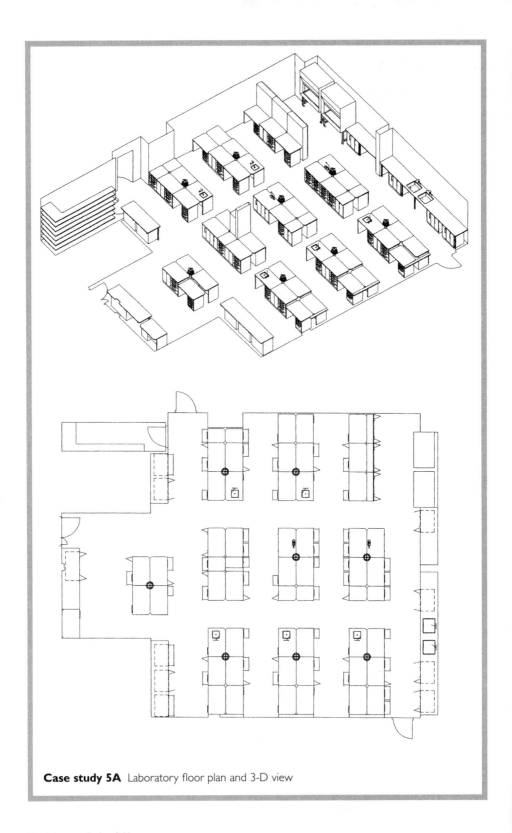

Case study 5A Laboratory floor plan and 3-D view

Case study 6

Life Sciences Building
Ciba Pharmaceuticals Division
Summit, New Jersey, USA

Architects   Mitchell/Giurgola Architects
         Partner in charge   Jan Keane FAIA
         Laboratory Consultant   Earl Walls Associates

The new Life Sciences Building consolidates research on a single R&D campus for the first time. The stepped plan organises a series of shared outdoor spaces to create a unified research area which is open and pedestrian in scale. The building is designed on a modular grid to accommodate a variety of disciplines and to facilitate adaptation.

To make the laboratories both flexible and open, and to promote interaction, there are very few dividing walls. The perimeter corridors have glazing into the laboratories above desk height and large windows to the outside, or are open into two interior covered atria. At both ends of these covered courts are circulation nodes with meeting rooms, stairs, elevators, and coffee break areas. The Ciba research group believes that new ideas in research often result from informal interaction.

The use of 88-foot trusses allows column-free laboratories with 8-foot interstices above. Services drop to the laboratories through openings in the concrete ceiling.

This project was awarded *R&D* magazine's Laboratory of the Year in 1995.

Jan Keane, partner in charge of the project at Mitchell/Giurgola Architects, explained the theory behind the design. 'Science today is characterised by new technologies. But bringing in new technologies is a change. Ciba did not want that change to stop its scientists from working. Soon after they started moving into the laboratory, Ciba purchased new robotic equipment and some of the laboratories' work modules had to be changed and this was hardly noticed by the staff working there.'

The advantages of the interstitial space and the column-free laboratory floors won praise from judges for the *R&D* magazine contest.

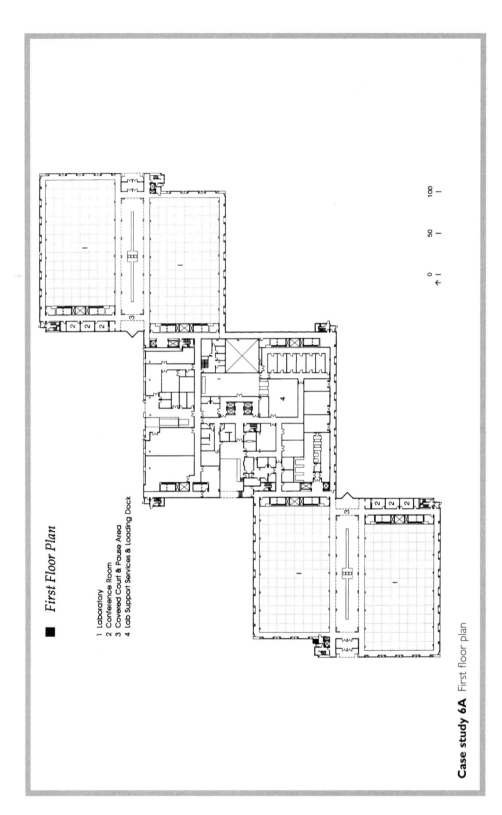

First Floor Plan

1 Laboratory
2 Conference Room
3 Covered Court & Pause Area
4 Lab Support Services & Loading Dock

Case study 6A First floor plan

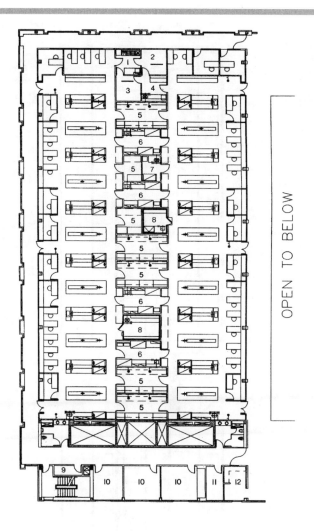

OPEN TO BELOW

■ *Typical Laboratory Layout*

1 Dark Room
2 Console
3 Scanning Electron Microscope
4 Preparation
5 Equipment
6 Tissue Culture
7 Isotope Room
8 Cold Room
9 Storage
10 Conference
11 Janitor's Closet
12 Vending Machines

```
    0    10   25        50
    ↑ I   I    I         I
```

Case study 6B Typical laboratory layout *(continued overleaf)*

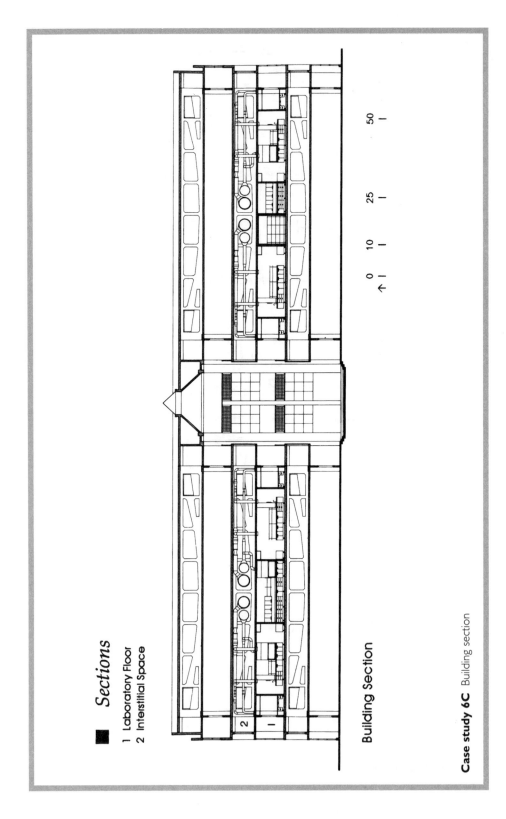

Sections

■
1 Laboratory Floor
2 Interstitial Space

Building Section

Case study 6C Building section

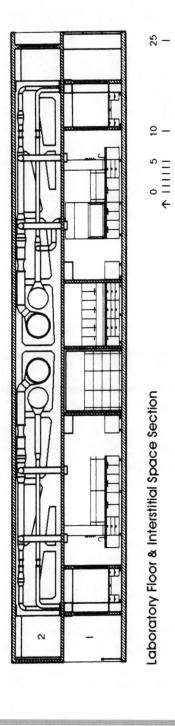

Laboratory Floor & Interstitial Space Section

Case study 6D Laboratory floor and interstitial space section

Case study 7

**Pacific Power Research Laboratories
University of Newcastle, NSW**

Architects   Jackson Teece Chesterman Willis
        Project Directors   David Jackson
                Damian Barker
                Ian Brodie

The Advanced Technology Centre for Pacific Power is a joint venture research facility with the University of Newcastle. Designed to accommodate 120 research and administrative staff, it provides 7000 m² of flexible, serviceable, adaptive space. This is not only a wonderful work place, it is a fully integrated design displaying high levels of energy efficiency, access and serviceability, safety and security.

It is a winner of the Royal Australian Institute of Architects' Environment Awards, at both state and national levels.

Energy efficiency

An essential ingredient of the brief was to design a building which demonstrates the efficient use of electrical energy together with solar efficiency, and protection of the natural bushland areas which adjoin the site.

Orientation of offices to the north maximises passive energy potential and outlook. With a deep floor plan, two storeys and a well-insulated roof, internal temperatures are kept very stable.

Natural ventilation for the entire building was investigated, however temperature variations fell outside the permissible for best functioning of the sensitive (and very expensive) electronic machinery to be housed.

The laboratories require the highest level of air-conditioning control. Their placement in the centre of the building provides a buffer all around to stabilise conditions. Separation of the write-up areas has reduced the area required for critical level air conditioning.

The air conditioning system installed maximises energy efficiency by using:

1 a computerised building management system;
2 a relief air system which uses economy cycles, providing unconditioned fresh air when outside temperatures fall within an acceptable range;
3 multiple air handling units addressing specific diversified needs, covering both time and intensity of use;
4 a night flushing ventilation operation which precools the structure during summer, using fresh air.

A building monitoring system has been implemented to audit ongoing energy consumption.

Lighting was a special consideration.

A fixed external solar control system excludes summer sun but admits winter sun for passive heating. Photo-electric cells activate to turn off perimeter lighting when natural daylight provides adequate lighting levels.

Light scoops introduce natural daylight into space deep within the office areas at both levels. Natural lighting in the public spaces reduces the requirement for artificial lighting to display highlighting only.

General office lighting is to a low ambient level to reduce the heat load in the building, with task lighting provided at workstations.

Access and serviceability

The building has been laid out to provide the greatest possible level of flexibility, for change to be able to be made to modify work areas, laboratories or overall expansion. The site gradient was used to provide subterranean accommodation for noisy, dusty and hazardous operations. This also enabled a level of secure car parking to be directly under the laboratories, giving unimpeded access to plumbing lines. The high roof space over the laboratories has catwalks for ease of access to the electrical and ventilation systems.

Safety and security

A safe and conducive work environment was encouraged by separation of laboratory and workstation areas. The pattern to movement of materials and hierarchy of spaces are clear in the floor plan. At the main level, stores line the southern face with the laboratories arrayed along the central band. These feed through to workstations and offices are along the northern face where advantage is gained of the views and sunlight.

This arrangement keeps safety to a maximum, and research staff spend as much of their time as possible in safe and attractive surroundings. The stores and laboratories are each surrounded by walls giving the appropriate level of fire separation.

A feature of the building is the dramatic stainless steel wall slicing through to divide the public from the private realms. To one side are the main entry and reception, which open onto an exhibition space and lecture hall. The 'silver' wall leads down to the staff lunch room, set apart from the work areas in its bush surrounding.

Security clearance is required to gain access to the world of research on the other side of the wall. Researchers can work unimpeded by uninvited guests.

(See also Plate 14 in the colour section.)

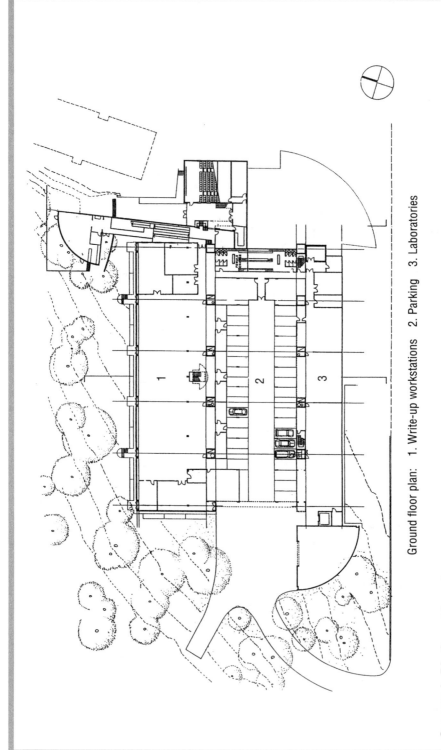

Ground floor plan: 1. Write-up workstations   2. Parking   3. Laboratories

Case study 7A Ground floor plan

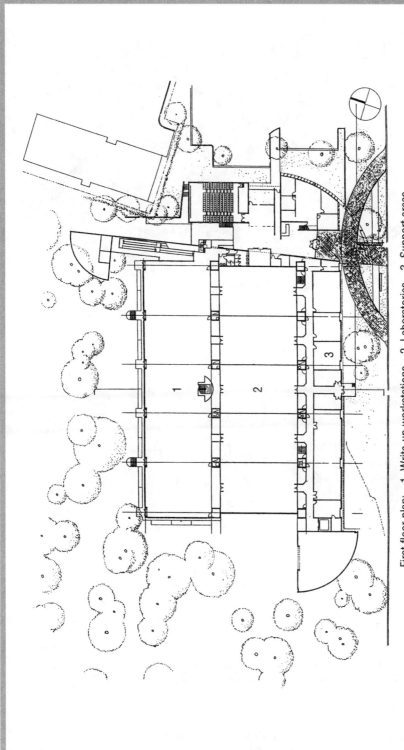

First floor plan: 1. Write-up workstations 2. Laboratories 3. Support areas

Case study 7B First floor plan *(continued overleaf)*

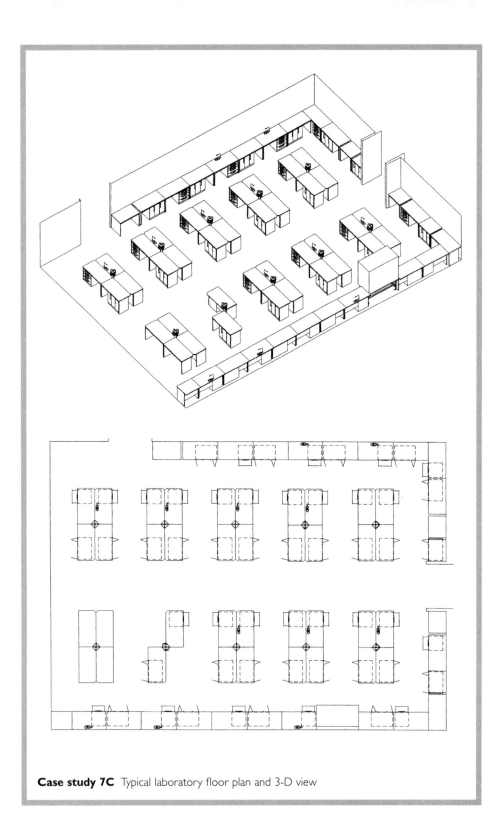

Case study 7C Typical laboratory floor plan and 3-D view

Case study 8

BHP Research Laboratories
University of Newcastle, NSW

Laboratory Design   Brian C. Griffin

This project was not completed but has been included as it is an unusual example in laboratory planning.

The staff currently work in a more traditional laboratory which is a long rectangular building. This does not provide the close relationship they desired between the staff groups.

The floor plan shows a design solution which is square, thereby achieving the closest possible relationship between each laboratory group. By locating the laboratory support facilities on the perimeter, the staff work areas are closely knit in the centre.

If one takes the view that the laboratories are a greater fire hazard than the offices, store rooms and other support areas, there is a safety advantage in this model.

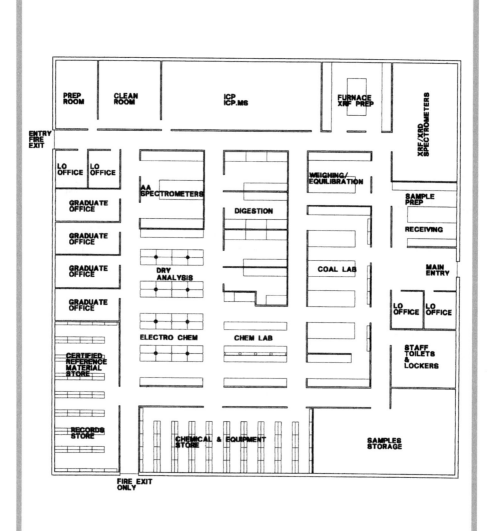

Case study 8A Schematic floor plan

Case study 9

Central West Pathology Services
Orange, NSW

Laboratory Design   Brian C. Griffin

This is a pathology laboratory in an Australian country city serving a population of 50 000, with 150 patients/day and a capacity of 350 000 tests/annum in biochemistry and 25 000 full blood counts/annum.

The laboratory groups had been accommodated in separate rooms and although the idea of moving into one open-planned laboratory did not appeal to the staff initially, they now agree that the shared space has many functional and social advantages. Microbiology is the only department given a separate space.

The photograph (Plate 15) shows an example of floor-standing equipment integrated with the workbenches. If the equipment needs to be relocated it is only a matter of rearranging the movable benches. The floor plan (Case study 9A) shows the spaces between benches for floor-standing equipment and an example of split benches.

All laboratory services are reticulated in a sub-floor space which incorporates a services tunnel extending to other hospital buildings, the gas store and engineering building.

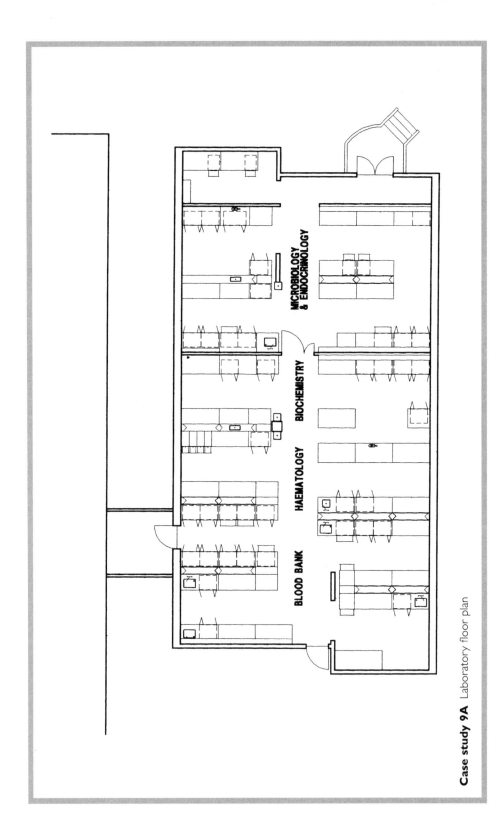

Case study 9A Laboratory floor plan

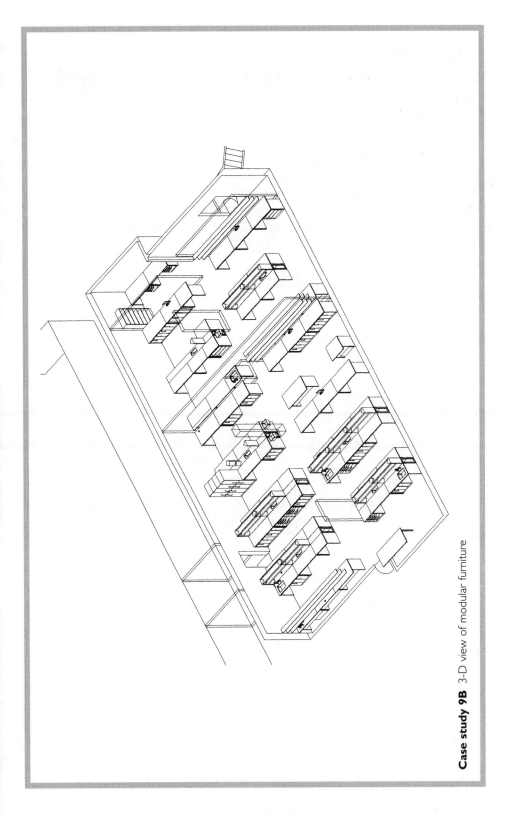

Case study 9B 3-D view of modular furniture

Case study 10

Commonwealth Scientific Industrial Research Organisation (CSIRO)
McMasters Laboratories
Prospect, NSW

Architects Collard Group Pty Ltd
             Project Director Peter Cook

The McMasters Laboratory has been designed as a generic laboratory building with flexibility to carry out a wide range of animal health research programmes in parasitology, molecular biology, immunology, histology, mycology, chemistry, biochemistry, pharmacology and information technology.

The laboratory is a linear two-storey building with an atrium entrance, is oriented strictly along an east–west axis to maximise environmental control and is planned on a 3 metre module to maximise rational planning. A central double-loaded corridor provides access to perimeter laboratories with a central spine of common support facilities including write-up, data capture, cold, hot and freezer rooms.

There is a central service area for media preparation, histology, autoclaves and glass washing and a central office area for administration with a seminar room and amenities. Emphasis has been placed on glazing internally and externally to maximise daylighting and safety observation.

Services including medical gases, vacuum compressed air and de-ionised water are reticulated in a fully accessible ring main system below first floor level, with risers and droppers to each floor with branches serving each laboratory bench.

A voice/data/power network is reticulated throughout the building and ducted to all benches. Reagent shelving above benches is removable so that bulky equipment can be bench mounted.

The internal environment throughout the building is computer monitored and controlled to ensure maximum energy efficiency.

'This is a very efficient building. It's also a very pleasant environment to work in'. Dr John Steel (CSIRO).

(*See also* Plates 16 and 17 in the colour section.)

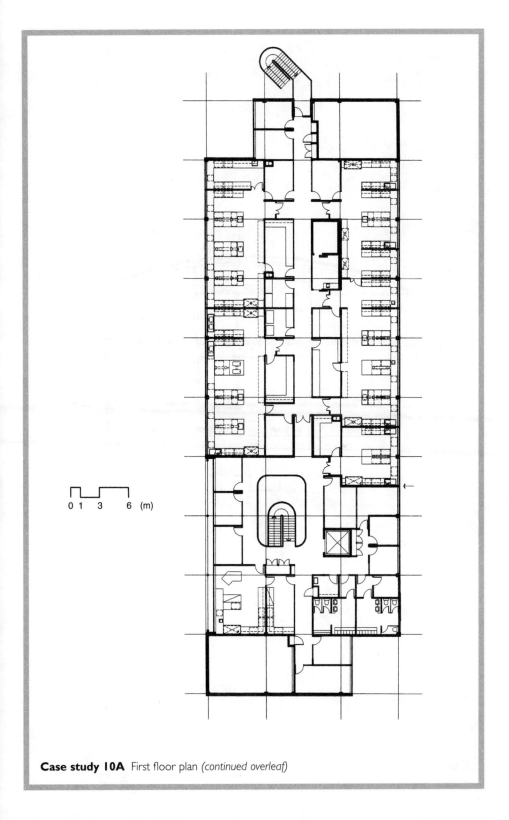

0 1 3   6 (m)

Case study 10A First floor plan *(continued overleaf)*

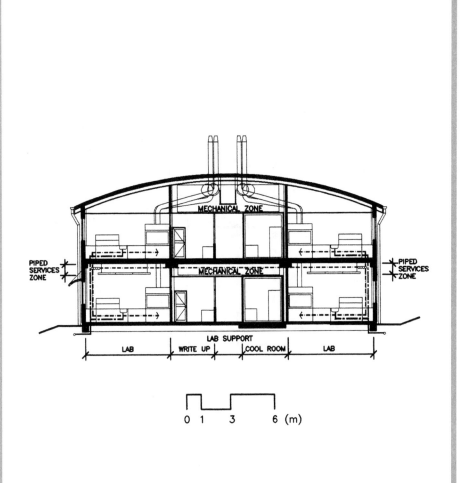

MECHANICAL ZONE

PIPED
SERVICES
ZONE

MECHANICAL ZONE

PIPED
SERVICES
ZONE

LAB SUPPORT

| LAB | WRITE UP | COOL ROOM | LAB |

0 1   3   6 (m)

Case study 10B Section

Case study 11

Australian Nuclear Science & Technology Organisation (ANSTO)
Radiopharmaceutical Laboratory
Lucas Heights, NSW

Architects   Collard Group Pty Ltd
        Project Director   Peter Cook

The biomedicine facility at Lucas Heights is used by the research and development arm of ANSTO's Radiopharmaceuticals Division.

The single-storey building has a footprint of 1000 square metres with Development Laboratories located in groups on either side of Automation Laboratories with ease of circulation and with extensive use of external and internal glass.

As well as maximising natural light there is generous visual contact between facility workers, with attendant benefits in terms of both safety and professional interaction.

The centrally located Automation Laboratories provide the core function for scaling up products from the suite of Development Laboratories. The building also includes a clean room and quality control room for product despatch.

All internal walls can be readily removed or modified, benches are open and under-bench storage units are movable on the floor.

The heavy duty suspended floor is 1 metre above ground level forming a piped services zone for pressure services and drainage lines. This arrangement gives maximum flexibility for future service alterations.

Above ceiling level is a full-height service platform for mechanical equipment, fans and air filters, which is also readily accessible for servicing or modification.

'One of the real beauties of this building is its flexibility. We wanted a laboratory environment where we could carry out several different but interrelated functions and that is very much what this facility offers us'. Dr Andrew Katsifis (ANSTO).

(See also Plate 18 in the colour section.)

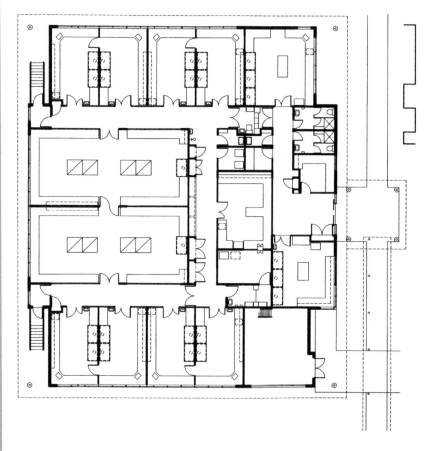

Case study 11A Laboratory floor plan

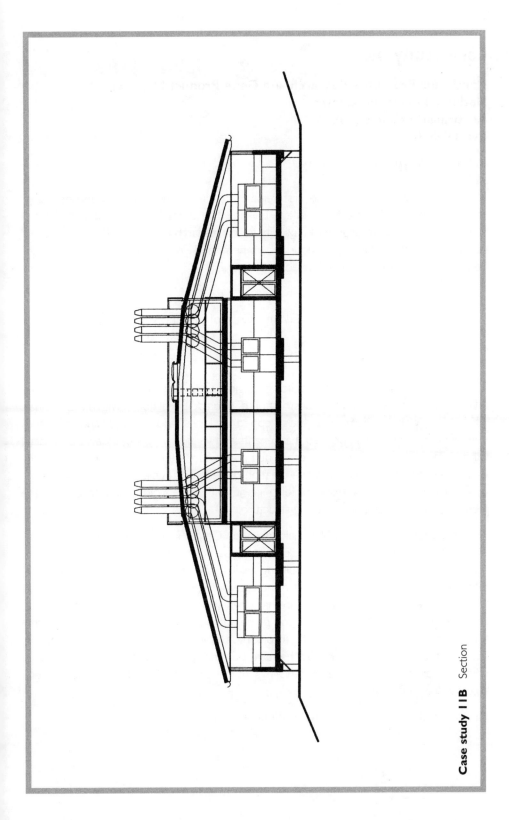

Case study 11B Section

Case study 12

Centre for Proteome Research and Gene-Product Mapping
National Innovation Centre
Australian Technology Park
Everleigh, NSW

Laboratory Design   Brian C. Griffn

This laboratory was one of the first tenants in this example of laboratories being accommodated within a listed heritage building. The client, Dr Ian Humphery-Smith, required the maximum degree of flexibility for his research facility. This was achieved by servicing the floor-standing robotic equipment and instrumentation on movable benches from services pendants fixed to the ceiling.

Architect for the National Innovation Centre   Crawford Partners
Project Directors   John Crawford
Alan Woodward

The 1907 single-storey heritage building, originally the New Locomotive Shop, was adapted to its new use with the construction of two additional floors, within the original fabric. The open atrium and the stepped galleries allow visual and acoustic communication between floors so that tenants and visitors are generally aware of each other's activities, able to see each other, bump into each other and communicate with each other on an informal basis. The creation of generous public spaces has not been at the expense of the historic building fabric with large voids enabling people to interpret and appreciate the existing structure.

The cost effectiveness of the National Innovation Centre is by all measures very good. The building rate/cost of $840/m^2, over a gross floor area of 8415 m^2, compares favourably with the cost of a new building fulfilling the same or similar functions. Cost effectiveness is 'value for money' and in the case of the NIC building one of the criteria to be considered is that a dual purpose has been achieved. The building's adaptation to new uses resulted in its restoration and preservation, hopefully ensuring its long-term future. There is an obvious difficulty in placing a dollar value on the preservation of heritage, however the sooner most heritage buildings can 'get a life', the less they will cost the taxpayer, and somehow this has to be brought into the equation when assessing cost effectiveness.

(See also Plates 19, 20 and 21 in the colour section.)

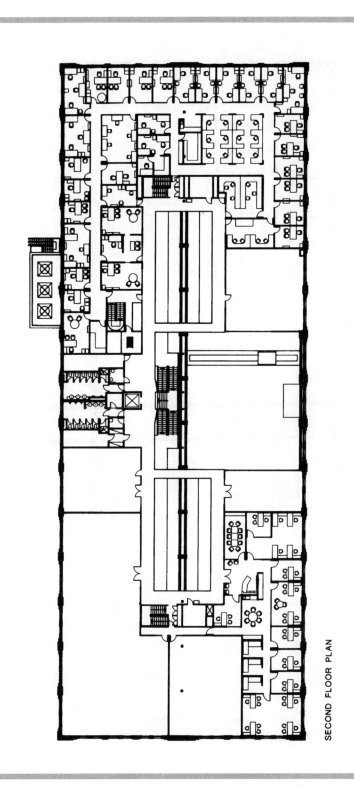

SECOND FLOOR PLAN

Case study 12A Floor plans (continued overleaf)

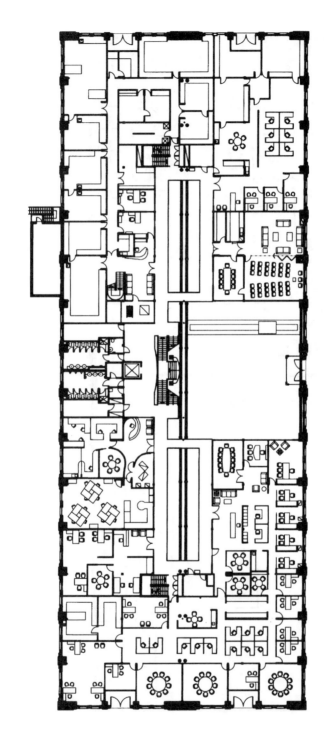

FIRST FLOOR PLAN

Case study 12A (Continued)

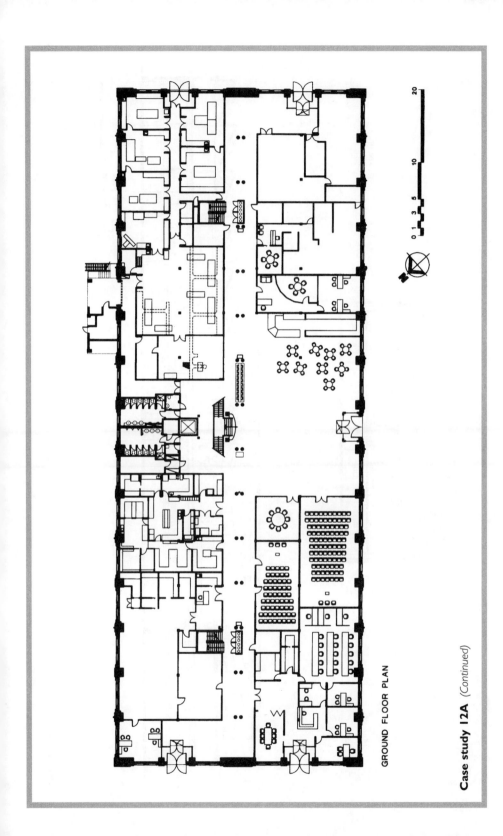

GROUND FLOOR PLAN

Case study 12A *(Continued)*

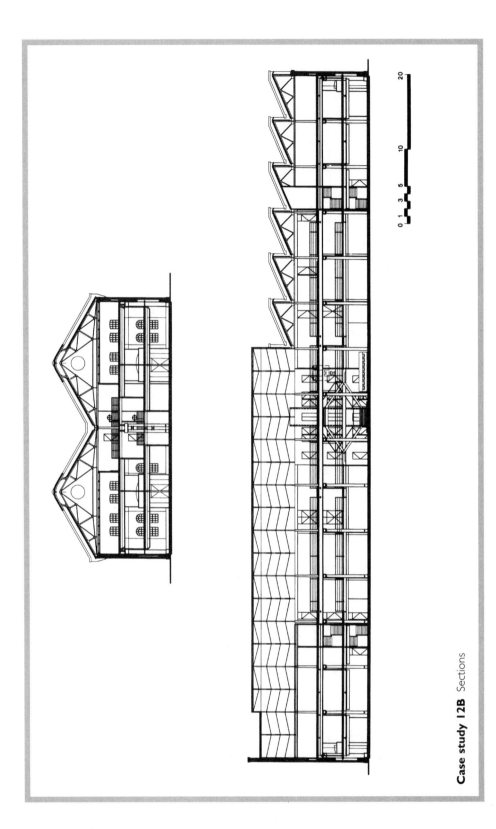

Case study 12B Sections

Case study 13

Garvan Institute of Medical Research
Sydney, NSW

Architects   Ancher Mortlock Woolley Pty Ltd
        Project Directors   Ken Woolley
                Dale Swan

The scientific research and support functions are bound together both visually and functionally by a gallery and atrium. Along its axis there are common meeting and display areas, lifts and stairs. This promotes a sense of unity and allegiance between the research groups and programmes of the Institute, and presents a comprehensible structure to occupants and visitors.

A 'double helix' open access stair links the lift lobbies and informal meeting space on all floors, its form symbolising the DNA structure, a central focus of this research facility.

From the atrium walkways the scientific activities are visible and each laboratory group can be accessed independently. The boardroom, where the future direction of the Institute is determined, is at the other end of the gallery looking over both the entry and back into the gallery.

The functional elements of the building have been given an urban presence, and internally the experience of the common spaces along the gallery and in the atrium are stimulating, encouraging an exchange of scientific ideas.

(See also Plates 22 and 23 in the colour section.)

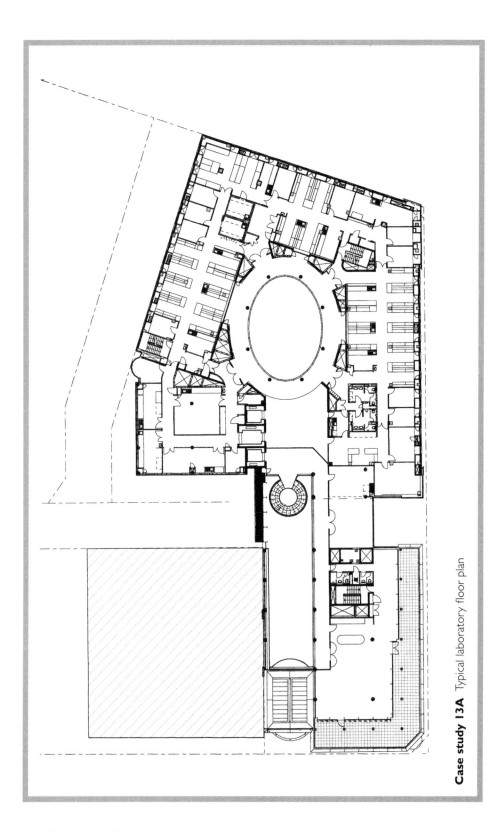

Case study 13A Typical laboratory floor plan

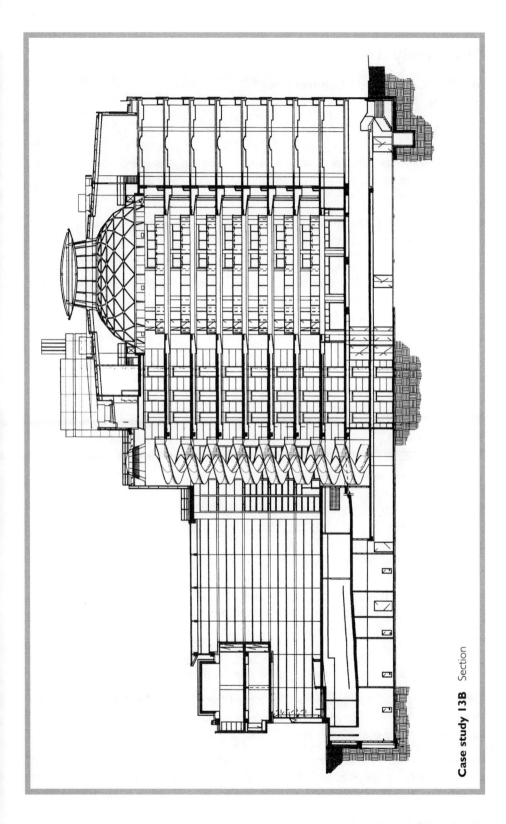

Case study 13B Section

Case study 14

ACTEW Corporation Laboratories
Fyshwick, ACT

Laboratory Design   Brian C. Griffin

This laboratory has been used as an example in the text as site constraints did not compromise the best design solution and the design process followed the methodology described in Part 2 – Design methodology.

Figure 2.3 shows the final developed laboratory floor plan which was used by the client to brief the design and construct project manager's team.

The seven laboratory groups have been accommodated in 'generic' facilities which can allow expansion and contraction of each group as future needs demand. The standard laboratory module of 3 metres and the standard modular furniture have been designed for all laboratory functions including support laboratories such as technical assistance and laboratory operations.

The central corridor plan allows the laboratory support facilities to be adjacent to the laboratories they serve.

The single-storey design, which is ideal for laboratories, has a sub-floor space for reticulating power, data, gases, water and waste services with easy access for change. The roof space is high enough for maintenance and accommodates all air-conditioning and fume extraction ducting and equipment. Ref. Fig. 3.1.

Architect for the design and construct contract   Bligh Voller
                                        Project director   Phil Page

Retaining Brian Griffin's basic laboratory modular layout, the non-laboratory functions such as the public entry, administration, conference, lunch room and library are accommodated in a separate building. This separation for fire protection regulation is a better design solution than a fire resistant-rated party wall as it allows windows to the whole of the laboratory perimeter.

The laboratory windows are protected from direct sun penetration by horizontal louvres as the orientation of the building is due north and south.

One of the many advantages of a single-storey laboratory building has been exploited very successfully with a continuous glass roof over the full length of the central corridor flooding the centre of the 'deep plan' with sunlight.

Primarily responsible for testing the city's clean water supply and waste water ACTEW are successfully developing business with the private community, particularly rural properties. To accommodate the expanding operations, planned second stage extension of the laboratory building will be achieved by adding further modules to the length of the building retaining the basic planning principles.

Stormwater is retained on the site in a decorative pond for irrigation to landscaping though not discharged into the town stormwater system.

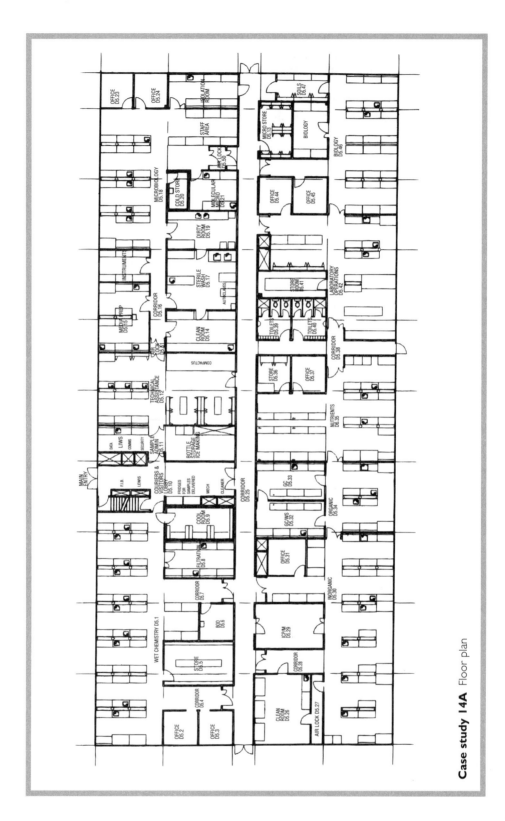

Case study 14A Floor plan

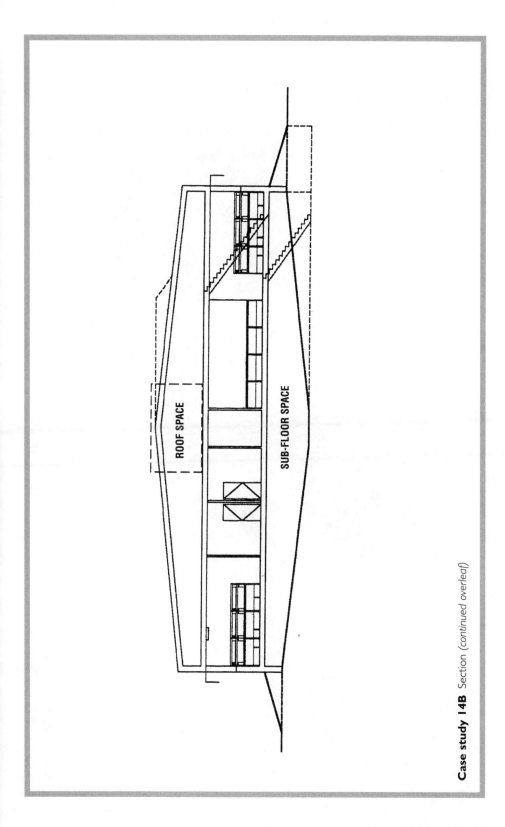

Case study 14B Section (continued overleaf)

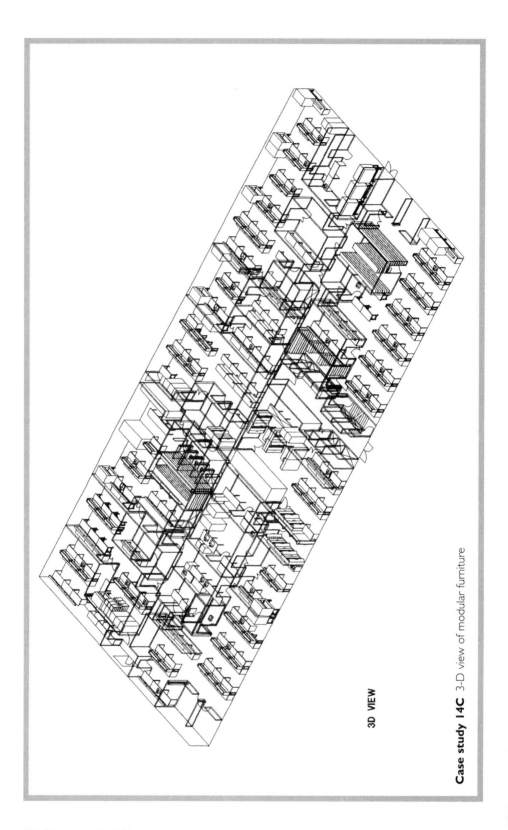

3D VIEW

Case study 14C 3-D view of modular furniture

TYPICAL
ASSEMBLY

FURNITURE
COMPONENTS

MOVABLE
REAGENT SHELVES

SERVICE BOLLARDS
ON SERVICE SPINE

MOVABLE
WORKBENCHES
BALANCE BENCHES,
EQUIPMENT, ETC.

MOVABLE
UNDER-BENCH
CUPBOARDS AND
DRAWER UNITS
AS REQUIRED.

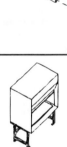

FUME CUPBOARD

BALANCE BENCH

SLIDING STORAGE
CUPBOARD

WALL STORAGE
CUPBOARD

Case study 14C *(Continued)*

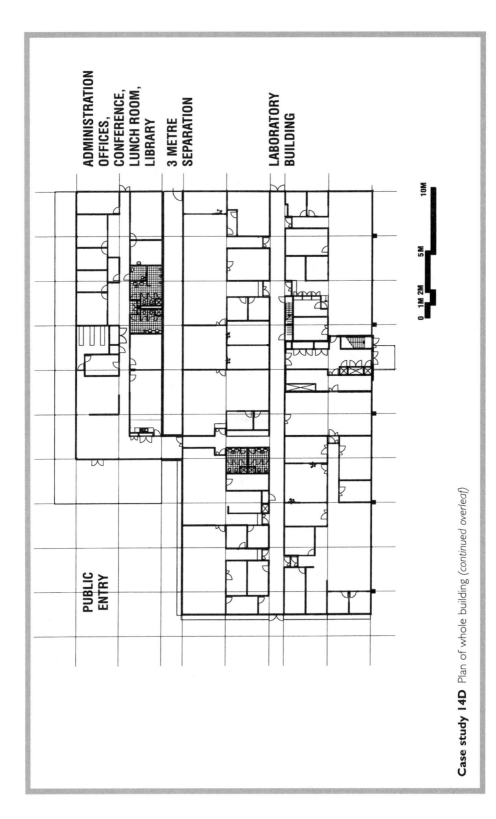

Case study 14D Plan of whole building (*continued overleaf*)

ADMINISTRATION
OFFICES,
CONFERENCE,
LUNCH ROOM,
LIBRARY

3 METRE
SEPARATION

LABORATORY
BUILDING

PUBLIC
ENTRY

0 1M 2M   5M   10M

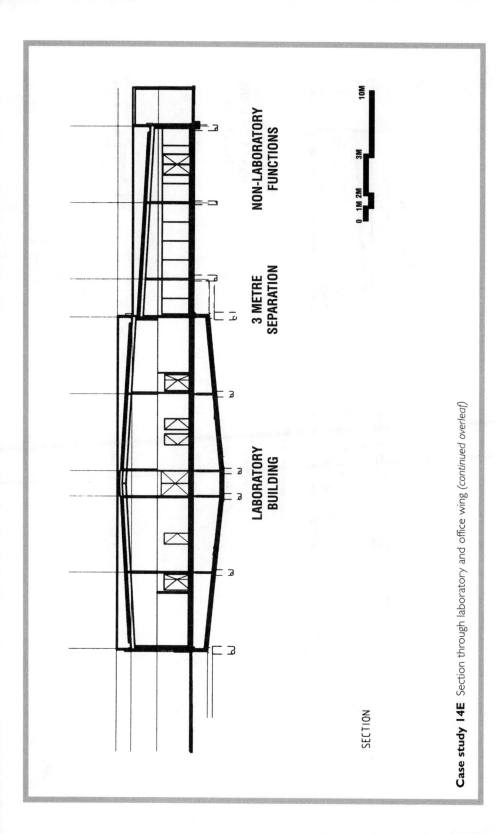

Case study 14E Section through laboratory and office wing (continued overleaf)

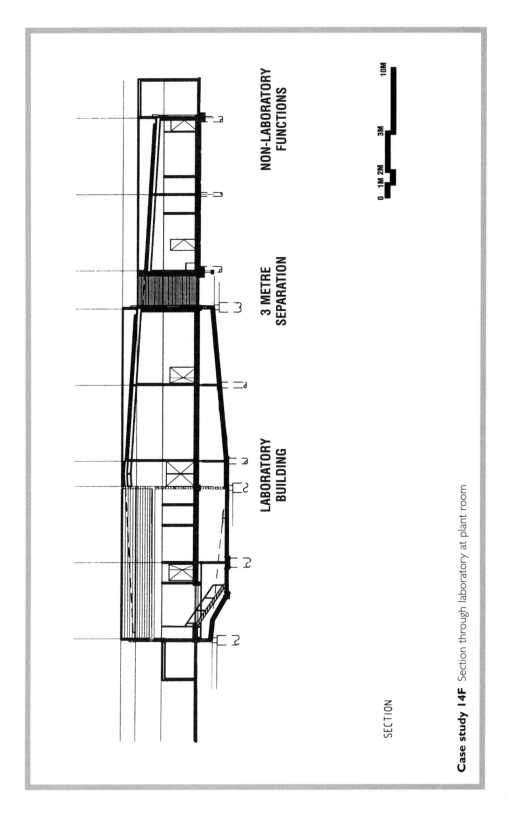

SECTION

NON-LABORATORY FUNCTIONS

3 METRE SEPARATION

LABORATORY BUILDING

0 1M 2M   3M   10M

Case study 14F Section through laboratory at plant room

Case study 15

Camelia Botnar Laboratories
Great Ormond Street Hospital, London

Architects   DEGW
             Project Directors   David Jenkin
                                  Michael Rushe

When the new facility was first contemplated, the client wanted the building to be an asset to the hospital estate. The plan was developed with flexibility in mind.

The five-storey building has been produced to suit its primary purpose – as a modern pathology laboratory, but the building is flexible enough to adapt to the changing needs of research.

Adaptability is inherent in DEGW's design, with its well-considered internal grid for ready subdivision, and a profusion of risers. This flexibility came about not as a response to commercial pressures but because, in common with almost all human activity, the nature of research has changed to one based on computer technology.

The floor plan is relatively simple, being divided into three longitudinal slices with the two laboratory zones flanking a central core and specialist area.

The core of the laboratories has a modest atrium which provides daylight in the centre of the deep plan building. It also creates a social focus and orientation point. Coffee bars on each level improve contacts between the various disciplines and departments – previously they were scattered across five sites. Transparent stair wells and small meeting rooms in the core also help in this respect.'

The two long span wings on either side of the central core provide column-free space for various combinations of laboratory and office. Risers are located at 6.4 metre centres and contain electrical cables, piped services, consumer units and space for extract flues. Service benches extend from the internal ducts and benches on the window perimeter wall are restricted to dry operations.

Running between the ribs are large, semicircular ducts constructed from silver powder coated steel. These are finely detailed with bands of small perforations for low velocity air. They contain integrated low brightness fluorescent luminaires, smoke detectors and fire alarms.

The director of pathology and all the users are apparently more than pleased with the results and the maintenance engineers have been complimentary about the layout and access to the services. An alteration exercise on the ground floor has proved that DEGW's planning grids are flexible and work well.

Bringing together all the pathology staff from five different sites has produced a big bonus for the hospital. The synergy of research and knowledge, with the routine work alongside research, has already spawned new ideas and fostered a new spirit of cooperation.

Extract from the *RIBA Journal,* June 1996.

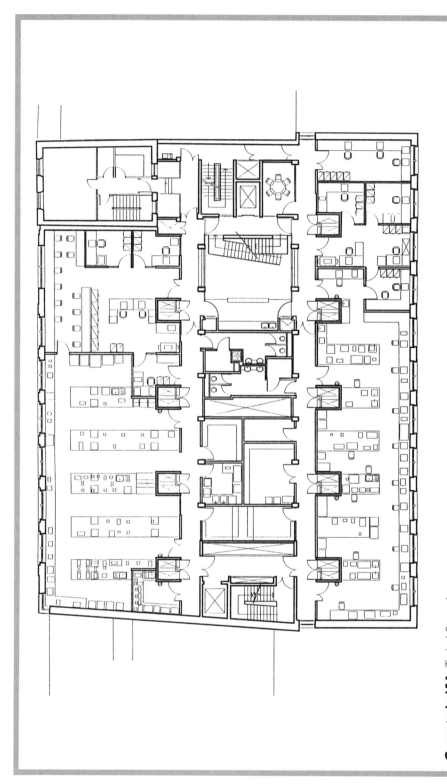

Case study 15A Typical floor plan

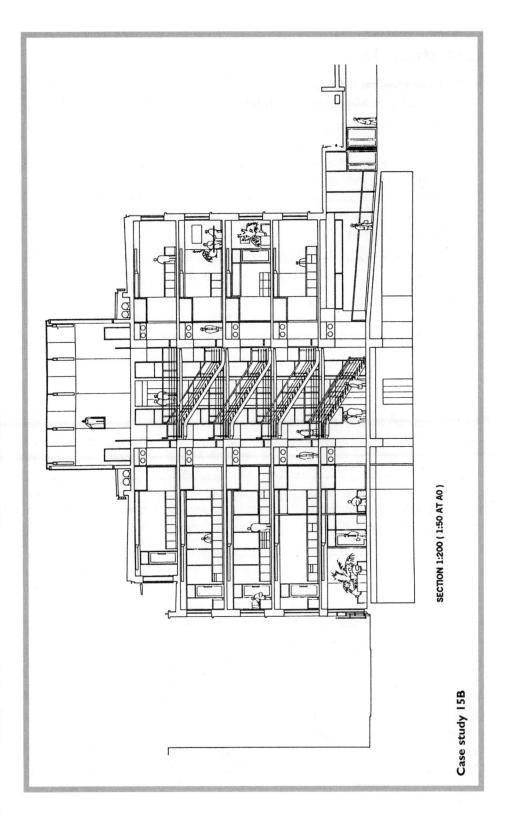

SECTION 1:200 (1:50 AT A0)

Case study 15B

Case study 16

Institute of Medical Science
The University of Aberdeen, Scotland

Architects David Murray Associates

The university wanted a 'research hotel', where research teams might expand or contract as funding comes and goes. The notion that a discipline should take residence for the whole life of the building has given way to the idea that different mixed-discipline teams will have to justify their occupation of highly serviced laboratory space, and that they may occupy it for varying periods.

As a result, the practice made flexibility the main priority, along with a respect for the choice of the occupant, and a concern for security and the environment.

The design is based on double-height laboratories interspersed with equipment rooms aligned along a corridor. On the other side of this circulation, offices look onto a full-height central atrium, intended to serve as the social focus for the whole building.

The ingenious section of the building doubles the offices above each other. The upper corridor allows maintenance access to the services, distributed along galleries over the laboratories, without disturbing the work below.

The high, naturally lit laboratories have a strong and dramatic spatial quality, solving the problem of maintaining visual control over the equipment and apparatus which is constantly changing. The researchers can alter the natural ventilation and lighting by closing blinds or opening lower windows, while a sophisticated building management system monitors and operates the upper windows and blinds. Fume cupboards and equipment with high ventilation needs are put in the equipment rooms which are cooled and mechanically ventilated. The mixed strategy is designed to optimise energy use.

The researchers can retreat from the labs to their offices to write up their experiments in a smaller, book-lined environment. These offices are ventilated into the naturally ventilated atrium. Again, the occupants can open or close the windows themselves. The offices look across at one another over the 9.6 metre width of the atrium. The occupants can see the activity at the entrance level, and communicate with people there, where photocopiers and coffee machines are located.

The space in the atrium is light and airy, the timber framing and panelling of the offices softening the bright white of the steel and blinds beneath the glazed roof. One of the major architectural contributions to the building, the atrium follows the success of similar spaces in laboratories designed by Venturi Scott Brown and Associates at Princeton, Pennsylvania, and Dartmouth – although the architectural language differs. The architect acknowledges a recent local building in the Aberdeen Science Park, by Michael Gilmour Associates, where small office/laboratories share a central roof-lit space aiding communication and cooperation.

Security is important in a building of this nature. Access is by swipe card, and on entering one is confronted with a cellular office for the reception staff. This office also contains the photocopiers, which seems to be a good way of ensuring it does not become sterile – front counter staff have a deadening effect on the entrances of many institutional buildings. Everyone has to use photocopiers, and if the coffee machines and other furnishings work well with this, it is possible that the building will encourage its users to meet across conventional departmental boundaries.

The atrium could become an anti-climax if not well managed and equipped. This space, together with the splendid conference room above the entrance, has potential to host promotional and public relations parties without disturbing the serious work going on elsewhere.

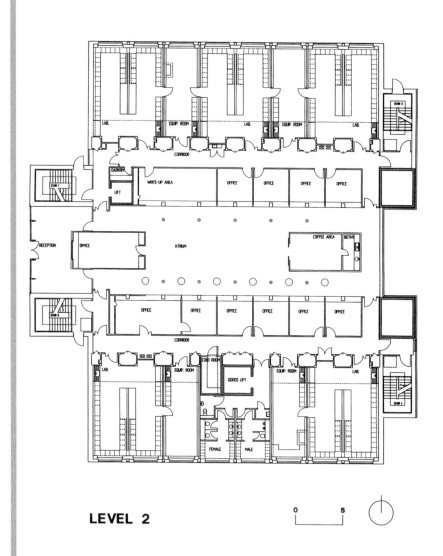

LAB | EQUIP. ROOM | LAB | EQUIP. ROOM | LAB | STAIR 2

CORRIDOR

CARRIER | WRITE-UP AREA | OFFICE | OFFICE | OFFICE | OFFICE

LIFT

OFFICE | ATRIUM | COFFEE AREA | BOTHY

RECEPTION

STAIR 3

OFFICE | OFFICE | OFFICE | OFFICE | OFFICE | OFFICE

CORRIDOR

STAIR 1

LAB | EQUIP. ROOM | COLD ROOM | GOODS LIFT | EQUIP. ROOM | LAB | STAIR 4

FEMALE | MALE

LEVEL 2

0   5

Case study 16A Typical floor plan

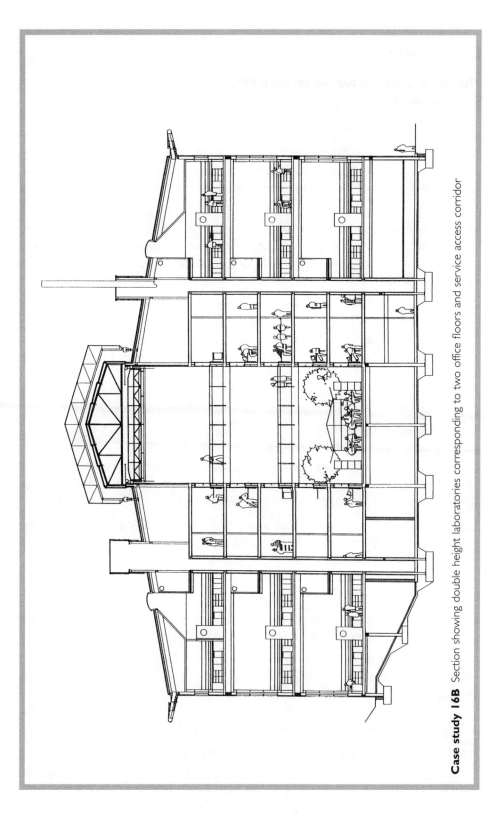

Case study 16B Section showing double height laboratories corresponding to two office floors and service access corridor

Case study 17

Therapeutic Goods Administration (TGA)
Symonston, ACT

Architect   Australian Construction Services

The Therapeutic Goods Administration (TGA) is responsible for ensuring the quality, safety, efficacy and availability of therapeutic goods which are basically medical products. The operations undertaken include premarket assessment, product quality assurance and education.

This is a significant example of a major government laboratory building of 18 000 m², half of which are laboratories. Because the site was virtually unrestricted it was possible to keep the building to a low rise not only for good laboratory design practice but also for limiting environmental impact.

The accommodation is on two floors but there are in fact five levels. The three additional levels are the roof space including air-handling equipment, an interstitial space between the laboratory floors and a sub-floor space including a part-basement. Air-handling equipment, filter boxes, air ducts, reticulated gases, waters and wastes are distributed between these three service levels to best advantage. This arrangement is the ultimate in services flexibility, allowing major alterations to serve laboratory alterations with virtually no disruption to the ongoing laboratory operations.

Being a regulatory authority, it is not surprising that safety standards have been a guiding influence on the building design. The floor plan shows six major compartments which are separated by fire-resisting construction. Each part is further divided into sub-compartments. In addition to the internal stairs which are used by staff during normal operations, there are external stairs for emergency use.

The floor plan of a typical laboratory compartment demonstrates the flexibility of the structural grid by half the compartment having a central corridor changing to a double corridor for the other half. From my experience the double corridors within the laboratories separated by a shared centrally located instrument laboratory are popular with staff and functionally efficient.

Another good example of compliance with laboratory standards is the sun control mechanism. Horizontal louvres on all windows are operated automatically by light sensors.

An example of the problems encountered when two or more autonomous departments are brought together under one roof is a consensus of opinion on the design of laboratory benches. As agreement could not be reached several different and non-interchangeable bench designs were installed. This has naturally reduced the flexibility which could have been achieved with a generic design.

The floor plan shows how the several departments have been brought together and architecturally the focal point is a very large atrium. In time this will also be a focus for social and professional interaction, when the laboratories are fully occupied.

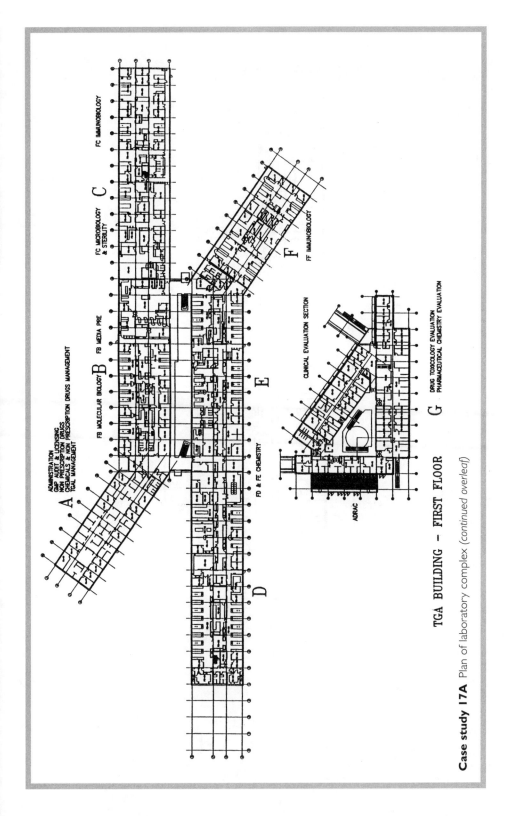

Case study 17A Plan of laboratory complex *(continued overleaf)*

TGA BUILDING – FIRST FLOOR

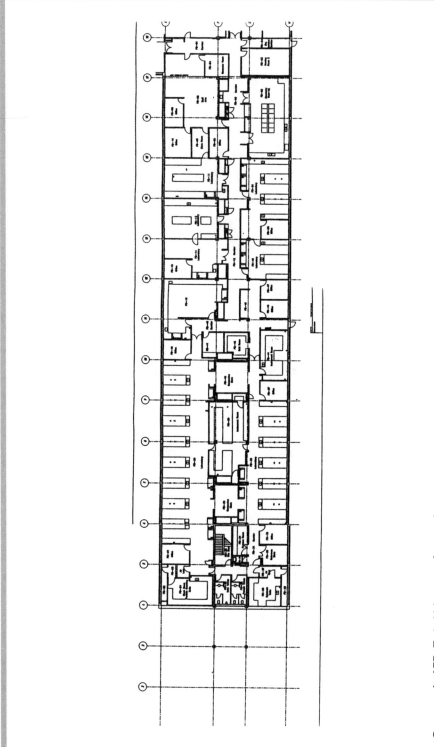

Case study 17B Typical laboratory for one department

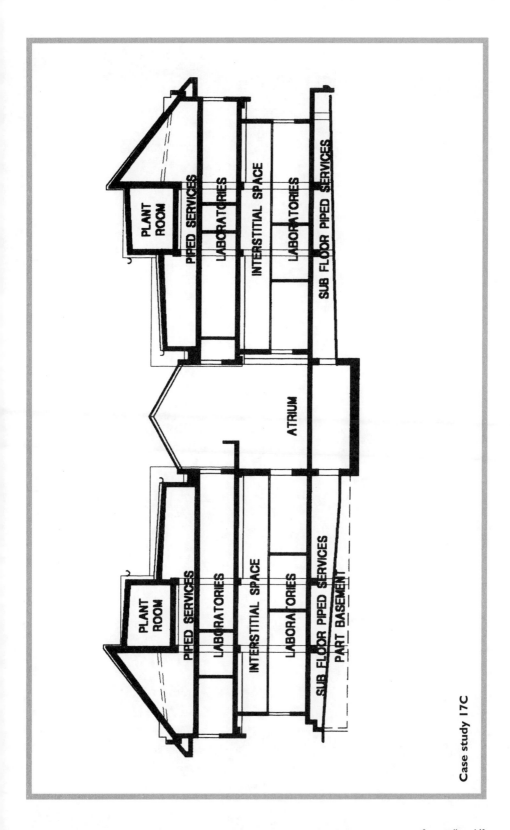

Case study 17C

Appendix A

Metric/imperial linear measurement conversion chart

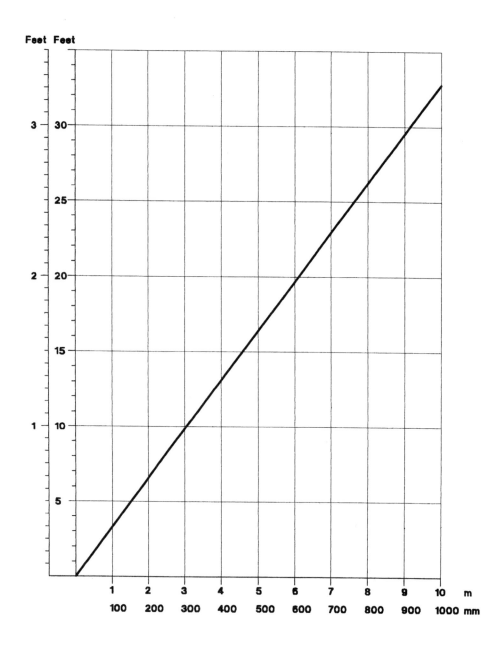

Appendix B

Design checklist

Site approvals from local building and health authorities and waste management.

Type and description of each laboratory and other functions.

Staff and job descriptions, including job locations.

Desired relationship between functions, including workflow if appropriate.

Hazards including description and location.

Equipment and instrumentation list including dimensions and location and service required.

Storage including shelf capacity and location.

Environmental conditions including acceptable range of temperature and humidity.

Staff facilities – first aid room, safety stations, lunch room, lockers, change rooms, toilets, showers.

Access for disabled staff and visitors.

Car parking for staff, couriers and visitors.

Security locations.

Building interior finishes – floors/walls/ceilings.

Laboratory furniture type, including bench top material.

Fume cupboards, laminar flow and biological safety cabinets, type and locations.

Local exhaust ventilation including canopy hoods, down-draught and lateral exhaust benches.

Specialist hazardous substance stores.

Bulk external storage capacity and location.

Laboratory glass washing facilities, autoclaves.

Compressed gas cylinder external store capacity.

Conference facilities

Appendix C

Typical design and construct programme summary

Stage	Timeline	Notes
Laboratory project feasibility study	▮	Including laboratory needs analysis, budget costs estimate, site selection and authorities approval
Project approved to proceed, budget set	✳	
Consultants selected and appointed	▮	
Client brief	▮▮▮	
Brief 'returned' and developed	▮	
Schematic designs	▮▮ ✳	
Selected scheme design development	▮ ✳	
Contract documentation	▮▮ ✳	
Tenders evaluation process and authorities approvals	▮	
Contract let	✳	
Building construction	▮▮▮▮▮▮▮▮▮	
Final inspections, equipment commissioning defects rectification, testing and authorities approval to occupy	▮	

✳ Project cost estimate reviewed at these stages

Appendix D

Laboratory hazards

This list is designed to assist in the identification of hazards, but is not intended to be comprehensive or exhaustive.

Mechanical:
vehicles, machinery, equipment in motion
compression/tension of parts
noise
vibration
firearms
pressure equipment (high/vacuum)

Radiation:
ionising
ultraviolet
infrared
laser
radiofrequency
electromagnetic field
extremely low frequency

Fire and explosion:
flammable substances
explosives

Temperature:
high temperature materials
cryogenic fluids

Hazardous environments:
confined spaces
working at heights
working at sea
working underground

Electrical:
high voltage equipment
live electrical equipment
static charge

Chemical/hazardous substances:
carcinogens
sensitising agents
corrosive agents
irritants
genotoxins (mutagens, teratogens)
toxic/harmful substances
generation of dust vapours, fumes
etc.

Personal:
manual handling including striking and grasping
slips and trips
fixed posture, e.g. microscopy
repetitive movements, e.g. keyboard
pipetting
pressure (diving/altitude)
heat/cold stress
working alone
mental stress

Biological:
biological materials
allergens
irritants
genotoxins
zoonoses
handling of small animals
handling of large animals

Appendix E

Laboratory building costs

While laboratory building costs do vary, the following two examples of buildings completed recently show the relative costs of the main components. Note in particular the high cost of the mechanical and electrical services. They represent 46% of the total single-storey building and 39% of the multi-storied building costs.

From my experience, the costs for mechanical and electrical services in budget estimates are generally inadequate and lead to problems later in containing overall project costs within the budget for the building.

Laboratory furniture is another underestimated item and generally should represent between 15% and 20% of the total building costs.

Example of single-storey building – 1500 m²

	A $ Cost/item	A $ Cost/m²
Building works	1 456 000	975
Laboratory fit-out	992 000	664
Mechanical and gas services	1 914 000	1281
Electrical services	510 000	341
Hydraulic services	364 000	243
Fire protection	49 000	33
Total costs	5 285 000	3537

Example of multi-storied building – 6000 m^2

	A $ Cost/item	A $ Cost/m^2
Building works	3 968 000	661
Laboratory furniture	1 800 000	300
Mechanical and gas services	2 700 000	450
Electrical services	1 900 000	317
Hydraulic services	700 000	117
Lift services	450 000	75
Fire protection	300 000	50
Total costs	11 818 000	1970

Further reading

The following titles have been selected and listed in chronological order to represent the progressive development of laboratory design. The most significant are those which were based on research into laboratory users' requirements and numbered 1 and 3. The Laboratory Investigation Unit (LIU) in particular, while concentrating on schools and technical colleges, nevertheless produced a wealth of reports (1–13) which significantly progressed the principle of flexibility in the design of laboratories.

1. Nuffield Foundation for Architectural Studies (1961) *The Design of Research Laboratories*, Oxford University Press, Oxford.

2. Asbel, Bernard (1964) *Laboratories*, Educational Facilities Laboratories, 'Bricks and Mortarboards', Report on College Planning and Building.

3. UK Government Departments (1967–1990) Laboratory Investigation Unit (LIU), Papers No.1, An Approach to Laboratory Building (1969), No. 13 Pathology Laboratories – design for tomorrow, and other LIU publications.

4. Ferguson, W. R. (1973) *Practical Laboratory Planning*, Applied Science Publishers Ltd, London.

5. Dreyfuss, H. Associates (1974) *Human Scale Body Measurements*, MIT Press, Massachusetts Institute of Technology, Cambridge, Massachusetts, USA.

6. Everett, K. and Hughes (1975) *A Guide to Laboratory Design*, Butterworth, UK.

7. Mills, E. D. (1976) *Planning Buildings for Education, Culture and Science*, Butterworth Pty Ltd, Australia.

8. Braybrooke, S. (1986) *Design for Research, Principles of Laboratory Architecture*, John Wiley & Sons Inc., USA.

9. Ashbrook, R. C. and Renfrew, M. M. (1991) *Safe Laboratories, Principles and Practices for Design and Remodeling*, Lewis Publishing Inc., Michigan, USA.

10. British Occupational Hygiene Society (1992) *Laboratory Design Issues. Technical Guide No.10*, H. and H. Scientific Consultants Ltd, UK.

11. Di Berardinis Associates (1993) *Guidelines for Laboratory Design, Health and Safety Considerations*, John Wiley & Sons, USA.

12. Cooper, E. Crawley (1994) *Laboratory Design Handbook*, CRC Press, USA.

13. Hain, W. Laboratories (1995) *A Briefing and Design Guide*, E. & F. N. Spon, London.

14. Mayer, Leonard (1995) *Design and planning of research and clinical laboratory facilities*, John Wiley & Sons Inc., USA.

15. Haski, R. (1992–1996) *Laboratory Safety Manual*, CCH Australia Limited.

Addendum

Most recent laboratory design developments

The development of automation and computer software for science has impacted on facility planning and design.

The two laboratory designs illustrated are recent commissions where the brief called for larger than usual workstations.

Laboratory staff now require the extra space for desktop computers, instrumentation manuals, project files, test records and other office type facilities apart from their laboratory benchwork.

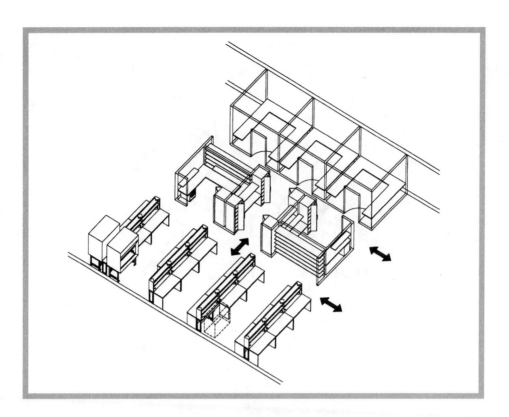

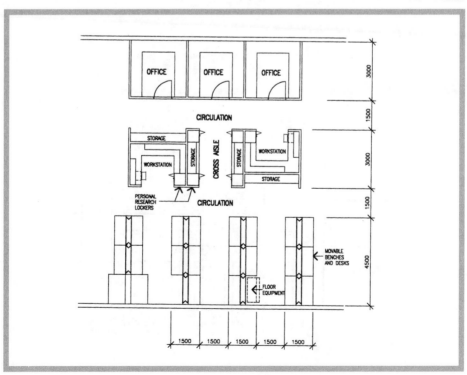

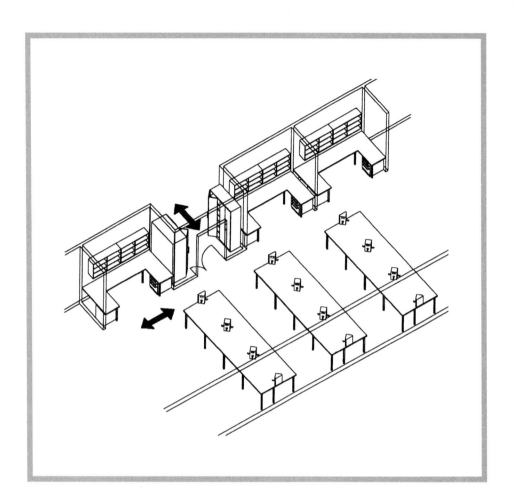

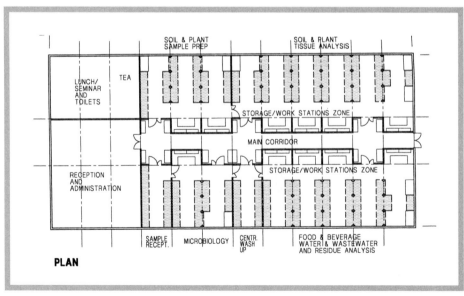

PLAN

Index

Readers should also refer to the Contents lists as some of those subjects are not included in this index. Those numbers appearing in bold type refer to the colour plate sections.

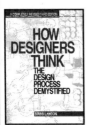